Jeannie Rose Field

Heart
Talk

Books by
Christopher G. Moore

Land of Smiles
A Killing Smile
A Bewitching Smile
A Haunting Smile
God of Darkness

North American Novels
His Lordship's Arsenal
Enemies of Memory
Saint Anne

Calvino Private Eye Novels
Spirit House
Asia Hand
Cut Out
Comfort Zone
The Big Weird

Non-Fiction
Heart Talk

Heart Talk

Christopher G. Moore

HEAVEN
LAKE
PRESS

Heaven Lake Press
P.O. Box 1029
Nana Post Office
Bangkok 10112 Thailand

Web site: http://www.cgmoore.com
EMail: chris@cgmoore.com

First Published in Thailand in 1992
by White Lotus Co., Ltd.

Second Edition 1998
by Heaven Lake Press

Printed in Thailand
Typeset by Jamie Zellerbach
Cover Design Michael Dougherty
Cover Photograph Richard Diran
Editor Gaynor de Wit

ISBN 974-8495-60-4

Contents

Acknowledgments
First Edition

Dr. Theraphan L. Thongkum, Department of Linguistics, Faculty of Arts, Chulalongkorn University, an internationally recognized linguist, devoted considerable time and effort to review the text. Also, Dr. Theraphan rendered invaluable advice in creating a consistent, romanized spelling of the jai words, provided the tone markings, as well as offered guidance, suggestions and assistance in preparing the glossary. Without her selfless help and advice it would have been difficult to have completed this book.

The National Association of the Deaf in Thailand for permission to reproduce the text and drawings which have been taken from The Thai Sign Language Dictionary, Revised and Expanded Edition (1990), with a special note of thanks to Dr. Owen P. Wrigley for his generous assistance and guidance in the preparation of Chapter 13.

Martin A. Perenchio, scholar and friend, for sharing his ideas and opinions about language, literature, culture, and history.

Khun Tuchmon Phonpiboonsoontorn, my Thai teacher, for her guidance and patience as I explored the rich landscape of jai.

Khun Kitti and Khun Ed of COMSET, masters of the computer and Thai language word processing programs, who diligently worked to successfully combine the English and Thai script.

Any remaining errors and/or omissions in this book are the sole responsibility of the author.

Acknowledgments
Second Edition

It has been nearly six years since Heart Talk was first published. The value of a second edition of any work is that it allows the author to reflect on how the first edition might be improved. I would also like to believe that the passage of these years as given me a greater understanding of the heart phrases.

The basic structure of Heart Talk has been retained. Each of the heart phrases has been rewritten, and the internal structure of each chapter broken down into sub-headings for ease of use.

My dear friend Shanker was kind enough to provide me with a number of new heart phrases that were not included in the first edition. I am grateful for Shanker's invaluable assistance in bringing new heart phrases to my attention.

My Research Assistant, Ratima ('Mickey') Sirsaard worked with distinction over many months in assisting me in preparing this edition. Her dedication, humour, and insight have contributed to making this a much better book.

In addition to Mickey and Shanker, many others contributed to this edition including Jampee Najomthong, Sunisa Najomtong, Nabthong Wetsanarat, Arunyanee Tangsinchayangkul, Ed Stauffer, John Hawker, and Norman Smith.

Translation and interpretation of any phrase is a highly personal venture. I do not profess to be a linguist. No doubt there will be those who will have their own views of the where and when to use a particular heart phrase and may not necessarily share my view. That is to be expected. The debate of usage is part of any book about language. What I do have, however, is a love of the Thai language, the culture and the people.

Heart Talk is the book that I would have liked have bought when I arrived in Thailand for the first time in 1983. I hope that others will be able to take away some small part of the texture, the ethos, the pathos, the humour, and grace found in the heart phrases.

Heart Talk
an
Introduction

Heart or *jai* is a powerful, pervasive, and complex metaphor. In Thai, you can experience and understand heart as black, cool, diamond, dry, fast hot, lost, open, merged, mixed-up, poor, tall, turbulent, wasted, wet or worried. While metaphors are the staple of novelists, poets, and playwrights, what is the relationship of heart as a metaphor to people interested in the Thai language and culture?

In *Metaphors We Live By* (1980) Lakoff and Johnson tell us that the "...human thought processes are largely metaphorical". Thus, whether you are a doctor, dock worker, lawyer, factory worker, merchant or jack-of-all-trades, then, you are pulling an oar in the same conceptual boat constructed from the same metaphors as everyone else in your language and culture. If you wish to row in the Thai conceptual boat, an understanding of jai is indispensable.

Many heart metaphors are universal such *cèp jai* or pain heart but others such as *kreeng jai* or awe heart do not travel easily across cultural frontiers. This book provides a "heart" guide to the human condition from love to hate, comedy to sorrow, hope to despair. The cumulative force of Heart Talk will help increase your awareness of how consciousness is shaped and defined in the Kingdom of Thailand.

The Thai language has the Thai word for heart in hundreds of different phrases. There is no single source in Thai or English where the heart phrases have been collected, organized and defined. One purpose of this book is to provide a light-hearted translation of heart phrases into English. While the first edition of this book contained approximately 330 heart phrases, this edition adds over 200 more in romanized letters and in Thai script, and a selection of 40 sign language Heart Talk expressions which may be found in Chapter 13.

In Thongchai Winichakul's *Siam Mapped* (1994), a book to be treasured for its brilliant insight into the Thai mentality, the concept of language is addressed in this way:

"As a prime technology of imagining nationhood, a language works a nation out in different manners—for example, by a spoken vernacular, the written language, the printing press, a court's language, a state mechanism like education, or the unified language of a colonial rule. In short, a language enables a certain group of people of their community an unprecedented, spatiotemporal definition. Nationhood is an imagined sphere with no given identity or essence; it is a cultural construct."

In this context, it should be added that heart talk phrases in the Thai langauge are another way of imagining the nationhood of Thailand, the identity of the people, a looking glass peering deep into the cultural heritage.

The translation of the Heart Talk phrases has been a very personal one. How we describe our feelings and emotions in any language is highly individual. Not everyone will agree with each of the meanings or the examples used to support a particular meaning (nor would I expect universal agreement). And I have been selective. Not every possible meaning or shade of meaning has been included.

The intention has been to write a book that readers will find enjoyable, provocative, and useful in their day-to-day conversations. It is a book that will prepare one to walk around the markets, shops, and streets of Thailand and communicate in spoken or sign Thai from your heart. It is a book which, in a short space, provides a number of insights into the Thai way of experiencing what an English speaker would call matters of the heart or, to take Graham Greene's title, *The Heart of the Matter.*

If the reader is a native Thai speaker, this book may help to create a bridge of understanding between the English and Thai languages. As with any bridge everyone has their own idea of the right design and structure. Everyone visualizes the heart from a different angle or perspective. This book, if not exactly a perfect bridge, is a way of providing a language map to an English speaker who knows little about Thailand. It is not, of course, the whole story. But it is a start in the right direction.

♥

When a Heart Talk root phrase is combined with the Thai word *khwaam* a noun is created. For example, *sabaay jai* translates as the adjective form for feeling happy. *phŏm rúu sùek sabaay jai.* That is, "I feel happy." The same phrase can be turned into a noun: *khwaam sabaay jai*, meaning "happiness". The grammar shifts. You can "have" happiness; *mii khwaam sabaay jai. kaan* is another bound element, like *khwaam*, that will convert some phrases into a noun. Thus *kaan tôk long jai* is the noun for "decision", while *tòk long jai* means "to decide" or is the verb form. A number of Heart Talk phrases are adjectives. They represent a quality in another person. For example, you might refer to another or yourself by the adjective *jai ÒOn* or softhearted. Also, *jai dii* or good-hearted is an adjective that is a common expression in Thai to refer to someone who is a good person.

The negation of most Heart Talk phrases is accomplished by adding *mây* to a root phrase. For example, *mây sabaay jai* would translate as "not happy." With the addition of *khwaam* to form a noun or *mây* to create a negation, Heart Talk gives you a spoken and hand sign vocabulary of over 1,000 phrases which are connected with the heart.

To understand the importance of "heart" is to understand the Thai way of looking at themselves and life. *jai* in Thai means both "heart" and "mind". In the English language, these two perspectives, mind and heart, have become accepted as two categories. In English, either one employs words which suggest to the listener he or she is invoking the rational, logical mind to perceive the world or self, or one's words suggest the speaker has resorted to his or her emotional, nonrational side. Since the Age of Reason, English speakers have become accustomed to viewing heart and mind as different. A common perception in English is to divide left brain and right brain "thinking" as an explanation for conduct and vocabulary. In Thailand, the consequences of the post-Enlightenment tradition did not split mind and heart into separate orbits of perception.

Thus, to comprehend the world with your "heart" in Thai often overlaps into many different contexts which a native English speaker would not associate with the heart but only with the "intellect." The Thai language also is concerned with the intellect but the emphasis that the emotive way of seeing and feeling is not separate from intellect is an essential and important feature of understanding the Thai language, culture and people. The Thai is rarely at a loss for an exact "heart" phrase to express a feeling or idea.

Have we in the West lost our range of communicating feelings? What would it be like to have a language where hundreds of phrases treat the state of our heart and mind as one? These are two questions you may ask when studying the phrases and examples in Heart Talk. You may discover some aspect of yourself that has been surrendered, forgotten or neglected in English. That realization may bring a smile or a tear. Heart Talk may open up the vast possibility of feelings that lie beneath the surface of our rational, logical, empirical world.

♥

The Thai language uses *jai* or heart to generate meaning in many contexts. The Thai language speaker is raised to understand that *jai* is a word with hundreds of shadings, an ever-present force within daily language. It is an evocative word that echoes with a sense of emotion. A leading Thai scholar, Weerayudha Wichiarajote, has commented that in Thailand:

". . .the basic drive is to establish extensive networks of personal relationships [which establish] the basic motivational drives. . .for friendship, love, warmth and social acceptance. In general, feelings are counted more than reason. . ."

With this emphasis on feelings in Thai culture, the language of the heart assumes a place of central importance. In a social or business context, the native language of a person is the way she or he reacts to you, or your ideas. In English, the "heart" connotes a sense of romance or medical science: we fall in love with our hearts or have heart transplants. The word "heart" in English, though of importance, occupies a secondary position to the logical or analytical path. Or at least it appears so when compared with the diverse uses of *jai* in the Thai language.

The Thai language requires us to reevaluate the way we perceive reality, in the home, restaurant, bar, business meeting, or travelling on traffic-choked streets. If we seek insight into another language, culture and people, we need some clue as to the ways they react when challenged by an idea, thought, book, newspaper, TV, or in the street, conference room or parlor. Understanding the uses of the *jai* takes one into the private backyard of the Thai language; a place where ideas are shaped, feelings formed, moods transformed, and relationships sealed or split apart.

♥

Many Thai language books have been written that prepare you to buy a cup of coffee or ask for directions to the train station. This book has a different purpose. It is a short tour of the heart words which, in the Thai language, explain some of the reasons Thailand is known as the Land of Smiles. This book provides an introduction to the source of those famous smiles; and explains, in part, the cultural difference when someone from the West meets and interacts with a Thai speaker. The way we talk about (or don't talk about) matters of the heart exposes something about what we feel is important, true or otherwise about ourselves.

Some Heart Talk expressions are descriptive of the nature of a person: A person with an impatient nature is *jai rÓOn* and a person with a senstive nature is *jai nÓOy*. Other times the Heart Talk phrase is connected with an emotional state and not necessarily the nature of the person experiencing the emotion. Thus a feeling of panic translates as *jai túm túm tÔm tÔm*. Another feature is the reversal of order in certain expressions. Thus *jai dii* refers to the nature of a good-hearted person while dii jai refers to the emotional state of gladness. In a number of cases the switch can turn a negative feeling into a good personality trait. For example, *ÒOn jai* means weary-minded, while *jai ÒOn* refers to someone who goes out of their way to help others.

If you ask a Thai speaker to explain if they had ever experienced one of the states embodied in a Heart Talk phrase the answer may reveal a great deal about that person's past. Because for the native Thai speaker there is a stored-up library of feelings and experiences he or she connects with each heart phrase. These heart phrases can become emotional road maps exploring the terrain of another's feelings and the way language defines the nature of another's personality. But be prepared to have the same courage to reveal your own heart, your own feelings, in return. What Heart Talk does is to provide a key to what is locked inside us all: a yearning to understand how another person feels.

In Thailand position and presentation are not stage props; they are the drama. Every drama needs a script. In Thailand, in many instances, the script is drawn from Heart Talk. For example, position can mean a number of things, including social rank, your job, your education, or your family background. The expressions of Heart Talk allow for dramatic interaction between members occupying the same or different positions. The way people occupying their roles see themselves is found in the grammar of Heart Talk.

It is difficult for many foreigners to master spoken and written Thai. Heart Talk is a way to master a narrow range of the language, a 1000-phrase vocabulary of the heart. This is your how-to guide. It gives you the means to talk about and from your heart in the Thai language. You can ask questions about the heart in Thai and how, in the process of using Heart Talk, you may find yourself better equipped to express and understand a rich variety of phrases. In learning this new technique of language study and, with enough practice, you might begin to do what the Thai speakers do by instinct: look, evaluate, decide, react, and judge as if their heart and mind were one.

Phonetic Guide

There is no universally agreed-upon system to write Thai in romanized letters. The phonetic guide below has been suggested by Dr. Theraphan L. Thongkum, Department of Linguistics, Faculty of Arts, Chulalongkorn University. One of the modifications to this system has been to use the transliteration *jai* for the word heart, as this is the most widely used transliteration. Please note that the sign—
— which appears below stands for final consonant. For this second edition, Gaynor de Wit has made a number of useful additions to this guide.

Short Vowels

i	$\hat{=}$, $\hat{=}$	ue	$\hat{=}$, $\hat{=}$	u	$\bar{=}$, $\bar{=}$
e	เ-, เ-	oe	เ-อะ	o	โ-ะ, -
E	แ-, แ-ะ	a	-ะ, -ั	O	เ-าะ, -็

		ay	ไ-, ใ- , ไ-,ใ-
		aw	เ-า
		am	-ำ

Long Vowels

ii	$\hat{=}$, $\hat{=}$	uue	$\hat{=}$, $\hat{=}$	uu	$\bar{=}$, $\bar{=}$
ee	เ-, เ-	oe	เ-อ, เ-อ	oo	โ-, โ-
EE	แ-, แ-	aa	-า, -า	OO	-อ, -อ

		ea	เ-ีย, เ-ีย
		uea	เ-ือ, เ-ือ
		ua	-ัว, -ว

Consonants

p	ป	t	ต, ฏ	k	ก
ph	ผ, พ, ภ	th	ท, ถ, ธ, ฐ, ฑ, ฒ	kh	ข, ค, ฆ
b	บ	d	ด, ฎ	j	จ
m	ม	n	ณ, น	ng	ง

f	ฝ, ฟ	s	ศ, ษ, ส, ซ		h	ห, ฮ
w	ว	r	ร, ฤ		y	ญ, ย
ch	ฉ, ช, (ฌ)	l	ล, ฬ			

Final Consonants

Final consonants are those at the end of syllable or word; in spoken Thai only a few consonants are pronounced as finals, and these represent the written consonants as follows:

k   – ก, ข, ค, ฆ

m   – ม

ng   – ง

n   – น, ญ, ณ, ร, ล, ฬ

p   – บ, ป, ผ, พ, ภ

t   – จ, ฎ, ฏ, ฐ, ฑ, ฒ, ด, ต, ถ, ท, ธ, ศ, ษ, ส

y   – ย

w   – ว

Tones

Thai is a tonal language and understanding the tones is an essential part of usage. The tone indicators used below are a guide to pronunciation. In Thai, using the right tone is crucial to convey the correct meaning of a word. The use of the wrong tone often causes confusion.

mid-tone (săaman)   a   (no tone mark)
low-tone (èek)   à
falling tone (thoo)   â
high tone (trii)   á
rising tone (jàttawaa)   ǎ

Pronunciation Guide

The following guide is intended to assist in translating the vowels and consonants represented by the phonetics used throughout this book. The attempt has been made to recreate the equivalent pronunciation of the Thai by using a familiar English word. Gaynor de Wit recommended this guide.

Short Vowels

i	as in tip
e	as in ten
E	as in tax
o	as in poke
O	as in top
u	as in foot
a	as in open 'u' sound, as in gun
ue	no English equivalent
ay	as it tie
aw	as in cow
am	as in come or gum

Long Vowels

ii	as in teak
ee	as in take
EE	as in fair
oo	as in low
OO	as in tore
uu	as in tooth
uue	as 'ue' above, but the tongue remains raised for a longer sound
oe	as in bird
ea	as in beer
uea	a combination of 'ue' and 'a' sound
ua	as in brewer

Consonants

b	as in bark, unaspirated
p	as in spark, unaspirated a 'bp' sound
ph	as in park, aspirated
d	as in dale, unaspirated
t	as in stale, unaspirated, like 'dt' sound
th	as in tale, aspirated
k	as in skate, also used to transliterated

the English letter 'g', unaspirated

kh	as in car, aspirated
ch	as in chat, aspirated
j	as in jet, unaspirated
m	as in male, nasal
n	as in nail, nasal
ng	as in linger, nasal
w	as in wee/wake/whale
y	as in you/yet
l	as in lea/lake
r	as in rake/rail
f	as in fee/fake/fail
h	as in he/hen/hale
s	as in see/sake/sail

Heart Talk
for the Good Times

Chapter 1

When you experience feelings of satisfaction, happiness, inspiration, relaxation or other pleasant feelings that create a sense of well-being, the phrases in this chapter provide a range of ways to express yourself in a fashion that is connected to your heart. In Thai culture and custom, it is from and through the heart that the language locates these feelings of well-being.

The good times and good feelings cover a wide emotional terrain, from getting what you wished for to being cheerful, satisfied, or at ease. You are not suffering or in turmoil or conflict. You are relaxed, happy, and controlled (or give that appearance to another) if you hear a Thai speaker refer to you by employing one of these Heart Talk phrases.

Appreciation

Pleased Heart

khrúem jai   ครึ้มใจ

khrúem òk khrúem jai   ครึ้มอกครึ้มใจ

When someone either gives another a special gift or bestows a favor, the recipient experiences a sense of pleasure or "pleased heart". This state of being pleased derives not only from the gift or favor but from the sentiment that the person who is giving shows that he or she cares about the other. The pleasure felt is by virtue of the act of giving. *khrúem jai* is the feeling of being valued by another person and the good feeling that comes from being appreciated by another. *khrúem òk khrúem jai* ("Pleased Chest/Pleased Heart") is another variation.

Contentment
Comfort Heart

sabaay jai   สบายใจ

yen jai   เย็นใจ

Use these heart phrases for the experience of feeling the absence of problems or burdens in life. The intellectual thought processes are turned off to problem-solving and problem-making. One has entered a state of feeling perfectly in tune with oneself emotionally—or a state of comfort and pleasantness. A person feels comfortable inside themself, with those around them and in their surroundings; there is an inner peace and sense of unity. Another usage is the feeling of contentment or happiness in the presence of someone else. There are no rough edges to the relationship; instead the personal connection is natural, fluid, and mellow. Alternatively one has eaten the perfect mango and sits back with a big grin, stomach full, heart comfortable.

Heart Home

bòek baan jai   เบิกบานใจ

sanùk sanǎan bòek baan jai   สนุกสนานเบิกบานใจ

A person's heart is where their home is. The Thais have great affection for their home. When someone feels cheerful and happy in their life then they are feeling *bòek baan jai* or "heart home". They experience the sense of their heart opening up like a lotus flower, with petals unfolding in peace, happiness and contentment. The essence is the overriding sense of well-being. When the heart is home, it is as if they are at home, too.

Relax Heart

yÒOn jai   หย่อนใจ

This experience arises when one emotionally withdraws from the woes and cares of the world. They disengage from their personal or business life in order to achieve this emotional state. Perhaps they had a fight or argument with their spouse, children, or a friend or had a conflict or problem in the office, or their car is working again, or their money has disappeared, but, despite all of this, they can go into their personal study, lean back in their chair, sip a glass of wine, listen to their favorite record, and read a book. They can relax their heart when others would feel discontent. As they withdraw from their troubles outside and close that world off from their heart, then they will feel *yÒOn jai*.

Relaxed Heart

phák phÒOn yÒOn jai   พักผ่อนหย่อนใจ

This heart phrase is used as verb when a person wishes to get away from it all. Often a person will seek refuge from the daily pressures and routines of work. He or she may wish to escape to Hua Hin in order to walk along the beach, enjoy the sand and sun in an environment free of obligations connected with work. Thus to *phák phÒOn yÒOn jai* might mean taking off for a long weekend to be spent upcountry after an intense week at work.

Satisfied Heart

kra yìm jai   กระหยิ่มใจ

The person who experiences this feeling of happiness or well-being has done something they desired. They bought a newly tailored suit or acquired a new computer system for the office, formed a new partnership for their export/import business or managed to keep their job in a period of economic decline. The feeling is one of being satisfied in having acquired an object of desire. For additional Heart Talk expressions for satisfaction see Chapter 10.

Trouble-Free Heart

plong jai   ปลงใจ

The term can be traced to Buddhist notions of putting concerns of the moment out of mind. This kind of person can stop worrying now and reside with happiness in the present. In business, in family, in his or her personal life the feeling of uncertainty or insecurity is absent. What had been the weight or burden of life on their shoulders has lifted. Their heart is at peace and they are at one with themselves and the world. A second meaning is that a person has decided, consented or agreed to perform (or not to perform) a task, favor or undertake an obligation.

Wet Heart

jai chúuen   ใจชื้น

This heart phrase is like *bòek baan jai*. A person feels *jai chúuen* when they are relaxed, positive, and in an upbeat frame of mind. There is a smile on their face and a spring to their step. The world is their oyster when they feel *jai chúuen*. People like to be around a person with a "wet heart" and are attracted to such a person's cheerfulness.

Chapter 9 is devoted to a discussion of heart phrases connected with self-control. In this chapter, one of the most frequently used and heard heart phrases is introduced. A more expanded definition of *jai yen* can be found in Chapter 9.

Convenience
Convenient Heart

sà dùak jai   สะดวกใจ

khlÔOng jai   คล่องใจ

Being put upon is one of the more unpleasant experiences of daily life, so convenience is much valued given the modern perils which consume a great deal of time and attention in the average life. Thus a feeling of convenience about an activity, such as it being the right time to go to work or to go out with a friend for dinner, has this heart phrase. Also, one can resort to this to describe a feeling of relief that comes from the discovery that there is no problem after the initial feeling of one on the horizon. One might believe that they are short of money to pay the rent, then they check their bank account and find a balance larger than they remembered. A person mislays their keys, then finds them under the newspaper on the dining room table. These examples show a sense of relief in the face of expected adversity and illustrate the emotions associated with *sà dùak jai*.

Convenient Heart

thanàt jai   ถนัดใจ

Convenience in this sense translates as skill or ease of accomplishment or use. Thus a person who plays the violin with great skill or a tennis player with a good backhand return feels *thanàt jai*. An employee who translates a complicated data base into English and who has the skill to do this task will also feel *thanàt jai*. The student who is able to easily answer all the questions on the final examination paper will possess a "convenient heart".

Desire Heart

yûa yuan jai   ยั้วยวนใจ

A person's impulses are triggered by the sight of something or someone they desire and they feel seduced by the object. It is viewing this seducing object which is the cause of *yûa yuan jai*. This object of desire--or what seduces--may be any number of temptations: From a beautful woman to a perfectly cooked chicken to a pot filled with gold. Or one may desire a ripe apple from a market stall, or a vintage bottle of French wine. The person or object which is *yûa yuan jai* acts as a seduction, and when confronted with the person or object one may try and remember *yáp yáng châng jai* or stop heart to control or restrain such impulses and desires.

Wake up the Tiger's Heart

plùk jai sǔea pàa   ปลุกใจเสือป่า

This heart phrase is typically used to describe sexually provocative clothing, actions, photos, words, advertisements, movies, etc. The long-legged starlet appearing in a beer or automobile commercial on TV is intended to "wake up the hearts of the tigers" watching the starlet sell the product. The desire is evoked through images, words or actions. The photograph of Mr. Universe pumping iron might wake up the tigers heart in a woman.

Pandering to the Heart

prà loom jai   ประโลมใจ

While the literal translation would be to comfort or console, the phrase has become associated with provocative images, words, and music designed to arouse sexual desire (or excitement) pander to the heart of the viewer, reader or listener. The source of such appeals may be from movies, magazines, books, TV, or cyberspace. Rock videos often employ erotic images indicating that the producers or promoters are pandering to the sexual desires of the audience, thus the rock video is *prà loom jai*, the movie is *prà loom jai*, and the romance novel is *prà loom jai*. An erotic calender is also *prà loom jai*. A person can also pander to the heart of another by relating an evocative love story. The story is *prà loom jai*.

Earnest
Dead in Earnest

jing jai yàang nÊEw nÊE   จริงใจอย่างแน่วแน่

When you feel totally involved or immersed in an activity or in your relationship with another person you feel *jing jai yàang nÊEw nÊE* or absolutely sincere. All other distractions fall away, and the full weight of your concentration is directed on the activity or towards the other person. This is a good feeling of being focused or concentrated. The phrase is used mostly for work-related activities or projects. At the same time, there is a downside to this state of being which carries a negative spin: Someone who has made a firm decision to do something wrong. The person who had concentrated his heart on stealing your new BMW may also experience this feeling of "dead in earnest".

Earnest Heart

dûay nám sǎy jai jing   ด้วยน้ำใสใจจริง

The feeling of giving something to another without any expectation of receiving something in return for the gift. Another person may help a friend in their work or studies. It is done out of the goodness of one's heart and not for selfish reasons. The person rendering the good deed would not accept money for his or her action.

Enjoyment
Full Heart

ìm jai   อิ่มใจ

ìm òep jai   อิ่มเอิบใจ

chûm jai   ชุ่มใจ

The heart is like a gasoline tank. Often it is running on half full or worse, it is running on empty. Instead of petrol, there are good feelings which top up the heart and let the body and mind run on a full tank. Thus, *ìm jai* is a general catch-all phrase to express a feeling of happiness at its peak. The expression comes close to the English notion of being contented. Completeness and depth of the feeling are important. The word *ìm* is normally used to say that one is full after a meal. Thus *ìm* alone refers to the full stomach and *ìm jai* the full heart—and with both organs filled the result should be a state of happiness.

Joyful Heart

phlòet phlooen jai   เพลิดเพลินใจ

râa roeng jai   ร่าเริงใจ

The state of being associated with an enjoyable heart occurs in those circumstances when one feels a sense of comfort, peace, or concentrated interest. Accompanying this feeling is a person's absorption in the moment—exterior distracting and annoying factors are filtered out and they are able to enjoy the moment totally and purely. The feeling is similar to *ìm jai*.

Entertainment

Entertain Heart

rûuen roeng ban thoeng jai   รื่นเริงบันเทิงใจ

A person who has an "entertained heart" is able to kick back, relax and enjoy an activity that takes him or her away from the multiple obligations of the day and/or the dreary routine of day-to-day living. What entertains is highly personal to each person. It might be a game of chess, a good novel, a walk in Lumpini Park, a walk along Kata Beach in Phuket, or a trip to Penang. In each case, the activity allows a person to enter into a state of well-being, enjoyment and contentment. And anyone who can assist in helping another entertain their heart is a highly prized companion.

Excitement

Amazing Heart

àt sà jan jai   อัศจรรย์ใจ

Just as one of the tourist promotion campaigns was called "Amazing Thailand Year", there is an "Amazing Heart" phrase that will survive any promotional campaign. There is an element of surprise leading to this state of amazement, which is akin to excitement. The catalysis may be an act of kindness, or receiving a benefit such as cash or gold. Another usage is connected to the happening of something strange or weird. For instance, if one's internet account is hacked, and someone reads one's personal mail, upon the discovery of this intrusion into one's privacy, the feeling of amazement would be one of the emotions felt.

Jerkily Dancing Heart

jai têen mây pen jangwà ใจเต้นไม่เป็นจังหวะ

Something has caused the heart to flutter or dance madly. This is the feeling of excitement experienced in relation to a person, thing or event. It might be the rush and thrill of an amusement park ride. Or it may be that Lek is so overwhelmed in meeting Khun Sorapong Chatri, the Thai movie heart-throb, that her heart starts pounding out of control. Vinai, who is a highly regarded and kind person, asks Noi out for dinner. She has had a secret crush on Vinai, so the invitation causes Noi to feel *jai têen mây pen jangwà*. Her heart is jerkily dancing about in her chest.

Fascination
Fascinated Heart

yuan jai ยวนใจ

There are people, things and events that charm others, and this quality of being pleased and fascinated is *yuan jai*. A person's attention may be focused on an artfully prepared Thai dish, a new suit, or the latest spy-thriller. They feel *yuan jai* in their relationship with these objects. In the presence of Miss Universe he or she may feel she is *yuan jai* by them. The feeling is one of attraction and desire. They are fascinated by that which they wish to possess. Other variations of the same phrase are: *yáw yuan jai* and *yûa yuan jai*.

Grace
Grace Heart

nám jai nák kii laa น้ำใจนักกีฬา

A literal translation would be athlete spirit. But this is too narrow as the essence of the heart phrases means the acceptance of any failure or defeat with a sense of grace and honor. In the context of sports, "grace heart" means good sportsmanship such as where members of a losing team accept defeat and shake hands with the winners. The heart phrase also has applications outside of sports. Someone who is passed over for a promotion and accepts his or her fate is said to have *nám jai nák kii laa*. Two competitors are engaged in a heated contest for a contract; after the winner is announced the head of the losing company shakes hands with the head of the winning company.

After One's Own Heart

sǒm jai núek   สมใจนึก

Most people harbor a wish or dream, and the object of this desire is longed for by the heart. The focus of attention may be an event, a thing, a state of affairs, or a person they want to come into their life. They are convinced the realization of this dream is good for them, is *sǒm jai núek*. The object of their desire may be a beautiful companion, a loyal son or daughter, a Rolex watch, a BMW, a scholarship, or dinner at a five-star restaurant. Whatever it happens to be, this is what they wish to come true.

Glad Heart

dii jai   ดีใจ
dii òk dii jai   ดีอกดีใจ

This is the emotional feeling of gladness. Gladness may arise in many circumstances, including when someone is getting their just deserts. If Lek is an evil and bad person and comes to a nasty end, those who suffered as a result of Lek may feel *dii jai* over his fate. If Lek is a loveable, kind, decent person and something good comes his way, such as a job promotion, those connected with Lek will feel *dii jai* for his success. Another person is *dii jai* for not complaining in the face of adversity, the show of patience or forbearance. To help another without an expectation of reward or favor are futher examples where this phrase is appropriately used.

Happy Heart

sùk jai   สุขใจ

The basic meaning of "comfortable heart", as in *sabaay jai,* applies to the definition of "Happy Heart." If your heart is comfortable, it is necessarily happy as well. Another lesson in Heart Talk is acquiring a comfortable, happy, at ease heart requires an extended vocabulary.

Heart at Ease

săm raan jai	สำราญใจ
preem jai	เปรมใจ

These are two more variations for expressing the feeling of a comfortable, happy heart. These literary phrases are mostly used in Thai writing and are not frequently used in spoken Thai. For the literal person, though, the occasional reference to "heart at ease" (in the appropriate context) will no doubt improve one's linguistic score card with a Thai speaker.

Like Heart

chÔOp jai   ชอบใจ

For most purposes, *dii jai* and *chÔOp jai* cover the same notion. If Lek is asked to go and see the classic film *In the Heat of the Night*, a film that she has wanted to see for some time, then she may feel *chÔOp jai* when she receives the invitation.

Overflowing Heart

tûuen tan jai   ตื้นตันใจ

Happiness and joy overflows the heart on occasion. When someone learns of the extraordinary efforts made on their behalf by another person they often feel *tûuen tan jai*. The person performing such acts of kindness does so at some personal sacrifice to themselves. Usually this feeling arises out of gesture within the context of a personal relationship such as between a parent and child, between lovers or spouses, or between friends. For instance, the daughter who has lost her job and has very little money spends what little she has left to buy her mother a birthday present. The mother, knowing the sacrifice her daughter has made, will feel *tûuen tan jai* by such conduct. The husband who has an important business meeting in Singapore but cancels the trip to celebrate his wedding anniversary with his wife. The wife will have an "overflowing heart" by virtue of his decision.

Uplift Heart

chuu jai   ชูใจ

To uplift another's heart is to say or do something that brings them happiness. Lek announces to her husband that she is taking him for a holiday to London, and produces the two airline tickets. He will feel *chuu jai*. The employee who receives a compliment from his or her boss will also feel that he or she has an uplifted heart. The lover or spouse who surprises his or her other half with flowers will likely inspire this state of happiness as well.

What your Heart wishes for

sŏm jai rák   สมใจรัก

Here the emphasis is not on one's personal dreams but on the dreams of others. Thus, one may wish another person to succeed in their efforts to achieve what they desire in their life. In this case, one feels *sŏm jai rák* for them, and support their desires in life by a display or expression of feelings of support for them. It is common to feel *sŏm jai rák* for one's spouse, lover, child or close personal friends. This state of heart is a powerful combination of emotional support and empathy offered to another as they pursue their quest for happiness.

Inspiration

Impressing the Heart

rOOy phim jai   รอยพิมพ์ใจ

A person who impresses another is *rOOy phim jai*. The person may impress with their wisdom, intellect, or talent. An object such as a beautiful painting is *rOOy phim jai* as well. The memory of a wonderful cool evening on Koh Samet with a loved one that lingers in the mind is *rOOy phim jai*. The impression may be for bad or good. The emotional imprint of the impression states locked in the heart.

Motivated/Inspired Heart

don jai   ดลใจ

ban daan jai   บันดาลใจ

rEEng ban daan jai   แรงบันดาลใจ

All three phrases are associated with motivation or inspiration. To inspire or motivate others to complete a task or accomplish a goal is the role of leaders, teachers, officers in the military and employers. It is their obligation to inspire those under their command, supervision or control to excel at their duty. By providing a good example, fair and just standards, and following through on what is promised, the soldier, the student, the employee, the voter will listen and follow. Inspiration may also comprise emotional support, guidance, insight and knowlege conveyed to others. Perhaps one sees a movie about a chess grand master and is inspired to learn the game of chess. Or one reads a book about cross-country skiing and is motivated to take up the sport.

Win Someone's Heart

chana jai   ชนะใจ

One may feel that they have won the heart of a friend, lover or employer, or they may feel that such a person has won their heart. A very diligent, hardworking employee will likely win the heart of his or her employer. A faithful, considerate and compassionate friend will win one's heart. Sometimes the winning over takes effort. For instance, the girlfriend's mother disapproves of her daughter's boyfriend, and the boyfriend, knowing of the disapproval, does his very best to win her heart. He may invite the mother to go out for a chinese dinner, knowing that she likes Peking duck. One can also win one's own heart in a struggle over doing the right thing. Here one decides to do right rather than taking advantage of another or doing wrong. The feeling of *chana jai* arises after this struggle is won inside one's own heart.

Relief
Relieved Heart

lôong jai   โล่งใจ

lôong òk lôong jai   โล่งอกโล่งใจ

pròong jai   โปร่งใจ

This is a state of being in which a person feels initially overwhelmed by feelings of panic, gloom or despair followed by relief. A passport, credit card or travellers cheques are misplaced. The distressed feeling of the time, trouble and expense required to replace such valuables suddenly vanishes once the article reappears. They may have an appointment with a friend and their friend arrives two hours late. The stormy emotions that build up during the long wait are released once the friend arrives. This sense of relief is the hallmark of this heart phrase. Their problem is resolved. Since the problem also resides in the heart, and to resolve the problem is to rid the heart of the heavy, negative feelings, to feel *lôong jai* means the heart has released the problem in much the same way a person releases a temple sparrow from a wooden cage. The sense is freedom and relief.

Relieved Heart

thŎOn jai   ถอนใจ

You haxve *thŎOn jai* or a feeling of relief at the end of a grueling Friday at the office. You feel relieved because the work that has occupied you all day is behind you, you can leave the office and enjoy yourself for the weekend. Used in this sense, the phrase carries with it a good feeling. This variation of "relieved heart" can also mean that you feel a fatalistic sense of throwing up your hands and feeling powerless over the situation or person. Perhaps you want your son to become a doctor and instead he has made up his mind to be a beachcomber. He won't listen to you. He simply goes off and lives on a beach, making a living picking up discarded bottles. Your feeling of powerlessness to stop him from this life choice brings your heart within the context of this phrase.

Security

Secure Heart

ùn jai   อุ่นใจ

ùn òk ùn jai   อุ่นอกอุ่นใจ

An emotional security comes when a person feels comfortable and the threat of exterior hardship appears remote. A person who receivcs a large monthly amount from a trust fund would feel *ùn jai*. Having salted away several million dollars away in the bank would be a cause to feel *ùn jai*. The soldier who goes into battle wearing an amulet or carrying a photograph of his wife or sweatheart would feel *ùn jai* by having the amulet or photo in his possession. Having a professional qualification such as a doctor, nurse, dentist, or computer programmer might have, would also bring this state of security. Presumably Bill Gates has an abundance of *ùn jai*.

When one is feeling at their most secure in life, then they will feel *ùn jai*. The degree of "warmth" in the heart is a metaphor repeated in a number of heart phrases. The sense of warmth, as used here, translates into a sense of security. If a person feels secure in his or her relationship with their friends, lover or parents, then they feel *ùn jai*. The operative emotional state is one marked by feelings of security, serenity and peace. On the other hand, to feel *rÓOn jai*, or "hot heart", is to feel angry and vengeful. If one feels *jai yen*, or "cool heart", they are composed, in control and collected in circumstances where a person who feel *jai rÓOn* might explode in a rage.

Heart Talk
for the Hard Times

Chapter 2

When you have a bad case of the blues or feeling out of sync with life, there may be no better language than Thai to express the extent of your emotional funk. The phrases in Chapter 2 cover a wide range of feelings experienced in various states of non-wellbeing. For example, there is a rich vocabulary of expressions for the many different states of sadness, depression, anxiety, doubt, worry, frustration, weariness, tiredness and fear.

The region of emotion also covers the feeling of unease, as well as the feelings of being disturbed, off-balance, lost, lonely, annoyed, impatient, hurt or lacking in confidence. Chances are you will find the right Heart Talk phrase to express the exact nuance of an ill feeling. A number of the phrases serve to describe more than a transitory emotional state—they are used to describe the nature or personality of a person. A person who is by nature tired, depressed, moody, bored or with a trigger temper may well hear a Thai speaker use one of the phrases in this chapter to describe his or her personality.

Annoyance
Annoyed Heart

khueang jai   เคืองใจ

In every relationship with others, there are conventions and rules to be followed, and when those conventions and rules are violated, someone may feel annoyed in their heart. For example, a person *wais* another and if that other person does not return their *wai* they may feel "annoyed hearted". Or after someone has stood in a long queue at the bank to deposit their pay cheque or at the post office to buy stamps, and after thirty minutes, the teller puts out the sign—gone for lunch—they feel *khueang jai* or annoyed. Though they have followed the convention, you have "lost out" and the heart goes into an annoyed state as a result.

Annoying Heart

nâa kuan jai   น่ากวนใจ

Someone is offering unwanted attention to another. The person who persists in such conduct after being told he or she should stop is *nâa kuan jai*. Lek is trying to study in the library or to work at her desk in the office and someone keeps interrupting her with an invitation for a conversation. Lek feels frustrated by this person's constant interruptions and tells him to stop. He or she continues to interrupt. Such a person has an "annoying heart".

Small Heart

jai nÓOy   ใจน้อย

A person who has a *jai nÓOy* nature is extremely sensitive and may become hurt or sad more readily than someone else. Such a person may read into your actions or words motives which you did not intend, suggesting that you have made an unfair accusation or insulted him or her. Care must be taken not to speak carelessly with such a person or you run the risk of hurting his or her feelings.

Suspicious Heart

nà Eng jai   แหนงใจ

You have just finished a heated quarrel with your spouse, child, or friend and the feeling afterwards is one of *nà Eng jai*. The aftermath has left you in a state feeling a little angry, a little upset, a little annoyed. Unresolved doubts remain lingering in the heart. Here are a few examples of how such doubts may enter the heart. You may have battled with your spouse over the issue of how best to discipline your child when she or he comes home from school late, and neither you nor her share the same point of view. You may have fought without satisfactory resolution with your child over the amount of time he or she spends watching television, talking on the telephone with friends, or surfing on the internet. You may have quarreled with a friend over her failure to repay you the money she has owed you for the last three months and are suspicious of her renewed promise to pay you tomorrow.

Wobbling Heart

jai wÔOk wÊEk ใจวอกแวก

Something or someone has disturbed one's concentration or distracted them. In such a case they experience the feeling of being annoyed: The neighbor's dog barks nonstop at two in the morning while you are trying to sleep, or the neighbor plays the latest heavy metal album cranked up to full blast on the stereo at three in the morning, or you are working on the computer and a power drill starts blasting outside your window—when one of these events occurs, then they will surely feel *jai wÔOk wÊEk*.

Anxiety
Alert Heart

wang weeng jai วังเวงใจ

This is a difficult heart phrase to translate. Alert only partially captures the meaning. Visualize a late night street in a dark neighborhood. One is alone on the street. In order to go to their destination one must pass a cemetery. The overpowering quietness of this moment in this situation creates a certain emotional state which the Thais call *wang weeng jai*. One's heart is on full red alert, waiting for some invisible force of danger or evil to make itself evident.

Anxiety Heart

hăay jai mây thûa thÓOng หายใจไม่ทั่วท้อง

A person with in this emotional state has some deep-seated worry or troubles that are on his or her mind. The emotional state is as if one's worries are so intense that they cannot draw breath. A person is riding their bicycle along Sukhumvit Road (not to be recommended) and a motorist drives too close, accidentally knocking down the cyclist. The cyclist's father arrives on the scene and he is an influential person and threatens to have the motorist sent to prison for a long period. The motorist, in the face of this threat and the powerful father, will feel *hăay jai mây thûa tÓOng*.

Boil the Meat Hot Heart

dùeat núea rÓON jai   เดือดเนื้อร้อนใจ

dùeat rÓON jai   เดือดร้อนใจ

This heart phrase is reserved for the big time personal worries. Someone is worried they don't have enough money to meet their daily living expenses and may have to go without food or shelter. In times of economic gloom, one has such a worried heart as to whether employment will continue. Without a job the car, the house, and the family disappear. The prospect of such losses would naturally cause extreme anxiety.

Hot Heart, Hot Chest

rÓOn òk rÓOn jai   ร้อนอกร้อนใจ

anaa thOOn rÓOn jai   อนาทรร้อนใจ

These two heart phrases are from an old Thai proverb. If a person walks around with a set of basic worries then they feel *rÓOn òk rÓOn jai*. The background emotional condition is akin to fear or insecurity. Someone is afraid that something will happen outside of their control and that he or she, or someone they love, may suffer harm as a result. He or she may fear that they will fail to complete a project assigned by their boss. Other examples include: One is afraid that their best friend will not recover from a major operation, or their child will fail in school, or their spouse will leave them.

Lost Heart

jai hǎay   ใจหาย

jai hǎay applies to the emotional state of feeling excessively frightened. The person is stunned by an unexpected event or thing. If, for example, one sees a ghost, this encounter leaves—unless they are a ghostbuster—one with a chilling fright or stunned. Or one discovers a burglar inside the living room at two in the morning with the family television under one arms and a knife between his teeth, then one is likely to feel *jai hǎay*.

Worried Heart

kang won jai   กังวลใจ

A worried mother, waiting for her child to return from school when he or she is late, may feel *kang won jai*. The emotional stakes causing the worry are less serious than *klûm jai*. There is, in other words, less to fear. Still the ache of fear is inherent in this emotional state. The emphasis is on the nagging fear that something bad may have befallen one or someone for whom one feels responsibility.

Worried Heart

klûm jai   กลุ้มใจ

In this emotional state, a person's feeling of worry may arise from a rapidly approaching deadline and they know there is insufficient time to successfully complete the task. Given the traffic jams in Bangkok, businessmen who sit in their cars, knowing they will be late for a multimillion closing which will fall through if they are not present, will feel *klûm jai*. A mother may feel that her daughter is doing something wrong in her life—perhaps associating with friends who smoke, drink, and hangs out in nightclubs with gun-carrying gangsters—and that the mother is powerless to stop her daughter from making a mistake. The mother may feel *klûm jai*. If a daughter would want to marry someone her mother disapproved of she would feel *klûm jai*. The tone conveyed is serious concern and represents the emotional state of anxiety or major worry.

Arguments
Conflicts in the Heart

tàang jìt tàang jai   ต่างจิตต่างใจ

She likes red but he likes blue and they agree to differ. Diverse minds often translates into diverse hearts. One says to the other after failing to change the other's mind, *tàang jìt tàang jai*. An impasse has been reached. Two (or more) people disagree about a subject but agree to disagree without changing their or the other person's mind. In theory, this is accepted without hard feelings.

Despondent Heart

jai hòt hùu   ใจหดหู่

jai hÒO hèaw   ใจห่อเหี่ยว

These twp phrases convey a lesser sense of adverse emotional feeling than *jai sĕa* or "Wasted Heart", but covers the same emotional territory that comes with feeling depressed. A person experiences or feels *jai hòt hùu* after some failure of purpose or plan. They feel despondent at the absence of an essential ability, trait, or characteristic that is regarded as necessary to cope with a situation or other person. A person who feels depressed may be viewed by his or her friends and family as *jai hòt hùu*. Another variation of "despondent heart" is *jai hÒO hèaw*.

Dispirited Heart

krà won krà waay jai   กระวนกระวายใจ

rÓOn rûm klûm jai   ร้อนรุ่มกลุ้มใจ

The person with a "dispirited heart" experiences feelings overwhelming despair and desolation. Often the experience falls on the heels of intense pressures of work, family and friends which combine to overwhelm the person to the point where they can not cope with the demands. A single event such as the receipt of a pink slip from an employer or an eviction notice from one's landlord will cause the employee or tenant to feel the kind of depression described by these two heart phrases. In circumstances where another person experiences depression caused by the crush of daily pressures or resulting from a decision or course of events outside of his or her control, either of these two heart phrases may be used to describe the emotional impact.

Encourage Heart

yÓOm jai   ย้อมใจ

chúp nám jai   ชุบน้ำใจ

This heart phrase comes into play when one is feeling a little depressed or feeling despair, and what a person needs is someone to brighten their spirits. The one thing in the world which will lift the cloud of gloom is to be cheered up. A person in such an emotional state looks to another to rally them out of their state of mild depression. What the Heart Doctor prescribes is *yÓOm jai*. Thus at the airport departure lounge, when one is struck with a bout of *sǎa kamlang jai mòt*, their travel companion pulls out a deck of playing cards, deals them a hand, and starts to tell them the story of when he or she was stranded for three days in an airport in Cairo. The playing of cards and the listening to the story slowly improves one's mood, the clouds lift and the heart is encouraged.

Shattered Heart

jai salǎay ใจสลาย

Lek sees her boyfriend walking along Sukhumvit Road holding hands with another girl. Vinai sees his girlfriend walking down the road with Lek's boyfriend, and he, too, like Lek, will have a shattered heart. In times of war if a child witnesses the execution of his parents by an invading force, he would feel *jai salǎay* for life. An upcountry woman who believes that she is going to work in a restaurant abroad but is forced into prostitution would also have a "shattered heart".

Tight Heart

kháp jai คับใจ

kháp òk kháp jai คับอกคับใจ

These expressions are used to convey an extreme emotional state of depression and despair. The husband whose wife has taken a minor husband might feel *kháp jai*. This is a question of temperament; what emotionally affects one personally with substantial weight may have less impact on another. A person who says he or she feels *kháp jai* may be signaling suicide. The tone of this expression is of major, serious bad feelings the person has trouble coping with. Such a person should be listened to carefully and assistance offered to alleviate this dreadful feeling.

Uncomfortable Heart

ùet àt jai อึดอัดใจ

tan òk tan jai ตันอกตันใจ

These heart phrases literally mean stiffled, obstructed or clogged heart and are used to cover feelings of depression or discomfort. A person feels uncomfortable through some sense of emptiness, lack of confidence, or failure. Also, they may feel uncomfortable in strange surroundings, or when they have a quarrel with a friend. The range of events, objects, feelings and encounters that cause feelings of discomfort are legion. Inevitably what makes one "uncomfortable in the heart" is highly personal to each person, and part of the exploration of other people is to determine zones of comfort.

Discouragement

Cutting of Courage Heart

tàt kamlang jai   ตัดกำลังใจ

Sometimes the loss of courage is inflicted by a remark or action of another. When one's girlfriend proclaims that her boyfriend is getting fat and bald, she has likely cut the courage in his heart. Such a remark might well cause him to lose his confidence (or *mòt kamlang jai*) and destroy his positive image. The employer who tells her secretary, Khun Vinai, that his typing skills are terrible may cause him to feel *tàt kamlang jai*.

Discouraged Heart

thÓO jai   ท้อใจ

The feeling experienced is similar to *ÒOn jai* or "Soft Heart". A child may wish that her or his father stop smoking and tries to convince him to cut down or stop but he continues his old ways. The father ignores the child's warning even though he knows about the health hazard. Later he dies of lung cancer. The child carries through life the feeling of *thÓO jai* about the past. The feeling is one of being discouraged. A good way to draw out another person is by asking them what in the past made them feel *thÓO jai*. There are bound to be old disappointments and failures bottled up from the early days, and these are stored in the heart. What discourages us defines who we are as much as what makes us happy.

Loss of Courage Heart

mòt kamlang jai   หมดกำลังใจ

One is disappointed or discouraged over the outcome of an event or with the views or opinions others have expressed about their performance, character or appearance. For example, one may have lost out on a promotion to a younger colleague. His girlfriend has told him that he is getting fat and bald. The political party she supported in the last election lost. After a currency devaluation he or she finds they have lost thirty percent of their buying power. In these circumstances, they may well feel *mòt kamlang jai*.

Lost Power of Heart

sǎa kamlang jai   เสียกำลังใจ

This the feeling that comes with broken will power. When a non-Thai speaker first learns to read Thai and finds great difficulty and the many long hours in sorting out the forty-four consonants, confusing *khor khwaay* with *dor dèk* (or the water buffalo with the child). In this process of starting over in a new language from the beginning, or reverting to a child-like level of language ability, one may feel discouraged or *sǎa kamlang jai*. A passenger may have been delayed nine hours at the airport waiting for their boarding call, and each time they ask the airline official for an update, she tells them the boarding will take place in fifteen minutes. They are likely to feel *sǎa kamlang jai*. They are ready to race, but there is no wind in their sails. One is without power in one's heart, and experiences motionlessness when what one desires is to move forward at full speed.

Lost Sympathy Heart

sǎa nám jai   เสียน้ำใจ

Your best friend made that special trip to a distant market to buy New Zealand lamb, then drove in heavy traffic to buy a bottle of imported red wine. When you arrive for dinner, rather than appreciating the efforts you have a negative reaction to the food. You announce: (i) you have hated lamb since you were a boy; (ii) the wine is of an inferior vintage; and (iii) you've already had a snack with some colleagues and you are no longer hungry. Given such an insensitive and thoughtless reaction, you should experience a spiral of emotions from your friend. One reaction, besides anger and frustration, is the feeling of being disheartened or *sǎa nám jai*. Someone has made an effort on your behalf and those efforts go unappreciated or are rejected. The sympathy of the heart felt for you soon vanishes in such circumstances.

Poor Heart

jon jai   จนใจ

The heart phrase might also be defined as "Baffled Heart." *jon jai* applies to the emotional state emerging from a personal failure to obtain something of value or to perform according to expectations. A person tries many ways to accomplish his goal of becoming a professional at golf and fails in each attempt until he is at his wits end. The person feels *jon jai*. The heart is impoverished as a result of the failure. The wife tries in many different ways to convince her husband to break off with his minor wife but fails. The wife feels *jon jai.*

Wasted Heart

jai sěa   ใจเสีย

A person who is *jai sěa* feels no confidence in himself or his abilities. His lack of confidence may be the result of a personal failure at work, the family, or in a relationship. The feeling that underlies *jai sěa* is one of being disheartened and discouraged with oneself. A related heart phrase with the same meaning is *jai mây dii.*

Disturbed

Absentminded/Floating Heart

jai mây yùu kàp tua   ใจไม่อยู่กับตัว

This heart phrase is used in circumstances similar to *jai lOOy* or "floating heart". An example is the person who cannot concentrate. Such a person has no attention span beyond a few minutes. The story in his or her mind shifts randomly, and he or she does not connect one event with another. This is not someone you hire to operate heavy machinery. Nor is it someone you want behind the wheel of your taxis from Don Muang Airport. *jai lOOy* is the expression used by an observer of such an unfocused person. Such an expression would be rarely used by the chronically nonfocused, unconcentrated person to describe herself or himself. It is important to distinguish between someone who sometimes has a "floating heart" and someone whose heart appears to be forever floating. The sense of focus and concentration inherent in this phrase is connected to the Buddhist concepts of awareness of what is what, and of being aware of what one is doing as they do it.

Child Disturbs the Body, Husband Disturbs the Heart

mii lûuk kuan tua mii phǔa kuan jai   มีลูกกวนตัว มีผัวกวนใจ

This heart phrase expresses the concern of many women (both single and married women) who have the demands of child rearing and looking after their husband's or boyfriend's needs and demands as well. Such a woman feels that the domestic pressures leave her very little personal time and freedom. This heart expression has become more common as women enter the workplace and have the same time constraints placed on them as their male counterparts, yet the traditional expectation of what is expected of women has not changed as rapidly.

Dejected Heart

jai khùn ใจขุ่น

A "dejected heart" often arises from the torments of others. For instance, teasing another about their personal appearance such as hair style, clothes, or accent. Hiding someone's keys or eye glasses when they are in a hurry to leave for an appointment may cause feelings of dejected heart in the person making the unnecessary search. The person performing such practical jokes or light-hearted acts of tormenting others may not understand that the person who is the subject of such acts suffers feelings of dejection as a result of such behavior.

Disturbed Heart

wûn waay jai วุ่นวายใจ

In this state of emotional turbulence, one is locked inside an emotional wind tunnel with the fan turned up full blast. One is mentally disturbed. Any number of incidents, slights, actions, moods can engage the rotary blades and stir up a terrible storm to disturb the normal equilibrium of the heart. What does it feel like to be inside such a place? One explanation is *wûn waay jai*—a state of internal rebellion against something or someone. One feels the full throttle of anger. A person can't sleep or eat. Something or someone is slowly burning a hole through one's heart.

Heavy Heart

nàk jai หนักใจ
nàk òk nàk jai หนักอกหนักใจ

When a person experiences the minor upsets of ordinary, daily living then their emotional reaction may be one of "heavy heart" or *nàk jai*. This is a good phrase to express the kind of minor hurt feelings suffered when another has let one down or left one feeling disappointed. In most cases, *nàk jai* is used in association with the hurt feelings caused when one discovers another person has put their self-interest ahead of the relationship with her or him. Their business partner may have taken advantage of them in a deal. Their child has been disobeying their wishes. Their lover tells them that her or his mother thinks the lover is too mean with money.

Neck Heart

jai khOO   ใจคอ

If one is feeling in a bad mood, then they have the feeling of *jai khOO mây dii*. The cause of his or her bad mood speaks volumes about their personality and state of being. Whatever the cause, once the foul mood strikes, those around them can expect *jai khOO*. This heart phrase is a good opportunity to explore questions surrounding personal disposition or mood. The neck of one's heart may go bad as a reaction to rainy season floods on your *soi*, their phone going dead in the office, or their driver causing an accident with the car. They may have received a rejection on a business deal or in a love affair.

Turbulent Heart

khùn jai   ขุ่นใจ

mǑOng jai   หมองใจ

This is hitting heavy emotional weather, one feels their state of being rocked from side to side. Someone or something has disturbed his or her emotional equilibrium. A client has cancelled an important appointment because he claims to be too busy to see them, and as a result the deal they have been negotiating falls through. They had no advance warning this was going to happen. As a result, the "turbulent heart" quickly go from a peaceful state to one of turbulence. The emotional wind tunnel metaphor is apt in these circumstances. In this emotional state, one feels suspicious of the motives of others who have caused one to experience a turbulent heart.

Doubtfulness

Doubting Love Heart

khaa jai   คาใจ

This heart phrase comes from a Thai love song and expresses the doubts felt by a lover. The doubt is likely to be focused on the degree of commitment to the relationship by the other person. The person who experiences the doubts may have some evidence that his or her lover is seeing another person. This suspicion would cause him or her to *khaa jai*. This heart phrase is used as a verb.

Doubtful Heart

khÔOng jai   ข้องใจ

This is a more serious feeling of uncertainty than *mây nÊE jai*. The wife may suspect that her husband has a minor wife. The feeling of not knowing whether her suspicions are true gives her a feeling of *khÔOng jai*. When haunted by feelings of doubt or when one believes another person is suffering from such doubts this heart phrase is a useful expression. It is a call for reassurance, of restoring trust.

Sudden Realization Heart

núek è jai   นึกเอะใจ

chalěaw jai   เฉลียวใจ

When a person feels doubt or uncertainty, then they have a case of *núek è jai*. A friend tells him or her that he would show up at the restaurant at seven for dinner. By eight, the person who is waiting glances at his or her watch, and notes the friend still hasn't arrived. They may feel skeptical as to whether he will keep the appointment.

Embarrassment
Embarrassed Heart

aay jai   อายใจ

lá aay jai   ละอายใจ

When a person feels that they have done something dishonorable or unworthy, and then later commit the same deed again, this causes him or her to feel embarrassed. There is often a lie, half-truth or deception involved. The act of being caught in a lie is a surefire way to be delivered to this heart state. In the middle of the night, having announced that he or she has stopped smoking, they sneak out for a cigarette. Their spouse or lover comes into the kitchen and catches them smoking. Two nights earlier when he or she found them smoking, and they promised an oath to never touch another cigarette. Having been caught breaking this promise, they may feel *aay jai*.

Full Heart

jù jai   จุใจ

A person has taken as much emotionally as they can. They have reached the upper limit, whether in an activity or inter-personal relationship, e.g., going to the pictures, playing a game, with their job, with their friend, spouse or child., or with government officials. They may feel played out. In disgust, they walk out halfway through a movie. Their boss shouts at them and after lunch they quit their job. A woman's husband has gambled away her's life savings and so she decides on a divorce and make an appointment with her lawyer. She feels the need to make a decisive move, a break, or to cut her losses. Such a person no longer have the ability to continue with a person or situation that has overwhelmed them. They have the feeling of being unable to take any more or can no longer be with someone. Other variations include *dàa jon jù jai* ด่าจนจุใจ for ("Scold until Heart is Full") and *lêen jon jù jai* เล่นจนจุใจ ("Play until Heart is Full").

Soft Heart

ÒOn jai   อ่อนใจ

This is the universal feeling of certain frustrations that bubble to the surface for most people during the course of ordinary day-to-day living; the trivial inconveniences such as the car that won't start, the phone that is engaged for seven straight hours, the constant engaged signal when trying to log on-line, the electrical blackout in a person's neighborhood for the weekend. One might see a man or a woman drinking too much at the bar, a little too quiet, eyes slightly glazed over in self-absorption and ask if he or she is feeling *ÒOn jai*. This is the sense of being weary in mind.

Impatient

Hot Heart

jai rÓOn   ใจร้อน

jai rÓOn applies to a person who has an impatient predisposition. Such a person may react negatively to standing in a post office queue, or waiting in traffic on Sukhumvit Road. In the extreme case, it may be one boxer bites off the ear of another. The "hot heart" reaction often is the verbal or physical outcome of a foul or bad mood triggered by an emotional upset. There are shadings to this phrase which are far less negative in nature and in these cases "hot heart" has more to do with a person's desire for perfection, quality performance, and refusal to accept second-best as good enough. Given this spin, a *jai rÓOn* person (of this type) may be a positive asset on the payroll. He or she has a temperament which demands that tasks and assignments are done quickly and demands quick reaction and response from others. More likely the lack of an easy-going nature, if this results on demands being placed on others, may lead some Thai speakers to judge the person as "hot hearted".

No Patience Heart

jai rew dùan dây ใจเร็วด่วนได้

The person who is *jai rew dùan dây* is not much liked or favored. Such a person violates one of the unwritten social rules: Always have a cool heart. The person with a "no patience heart" is likely to exhibit behavior which is greedy as well as impatient in nature. This person thinks of their own interests and ignores the interests or feelings of others. Such a person cuts in front of the queue at the bank or post office. Lek owns a small business and hires people to help her run it. After a couple of months, though, Lek is unhappy with the profits earned in the business and dismisses the non-productive workers in the factory. While this may make perfectly good economic sense, Lek would be criticized by the dismissed workers as *jai rew dùan dây* because she has not waited long enough for the business to take off. She has been impatient and unwilling to carry the workers through some bad times. Rather than support her workers, she has fired them so that she will have more money for herself.

Loneliness

Alone Heart

wáa wèe jai ว้าเหว่ใจ

"Alone Heart" express one's feeling of aloneness. Being alone in the heart comes from living in isolation from others, especially family and friends. The Thais are a social people and maintain close connection with their family and friends. Great value is placed on this social support structure. Someone banished from this nurturing set of relationships is likely to suffer from an "alone heart". Being alone is viewed as a negative emotional state and so it is not surprising there are a number Heart Talk expressions for the feeling of aloneness.

Lonely Heart

plìaw jai   เปลี่ยวใจ

The phrase is used to describe emotional states of isolation. A person is fed up with eating dinner alone, or sleeping alone night after night. They experience an empty, hollow feeling. And something wakes up inside them and they discover that they are all alone. With this realization comes a feeling of unhappiness or desolation arising out of the feeling of loneliness. Perhaps their spouse or lover has gone causing them to feel lonely. Maybe their spouse or lover is beside them physically but the love has vanished from the relationship. The use of the phrase may be a cry for rescue from this solitary state of being.

Powerlessness

Powerless Heart

mòt kà cìt kà jai   หมดกะจิตกะใจ

Something has happened or has been said that causes a person to lose his or her desire to deal with a situation. Emotionally, the condition is one of feeling powerless. Events are beyond the ability of the person to influence or control. There is a feeling of lack of will in the face of such paralysis. In this state (which often is merely temporary) the person loses any desire to go out with friends or to be around family. Such a person wishes to be left alone. For example, Lek has been given a notice of termination by her employer of seven years. She is devasted, knowing that there are few jobs now being offered because of economic problems. Having lost her job, she will experience *mòt kà jìt kà jai*. Such a person feels that they cannot no longer shape the events of their own life.

Sadness

Break Heart

hǔa jai thÊEp jà khàat   หัวใจแทบจะขาด

A person experiences an attack of *hǔa jai thÊEp jà khàat* when they feel that their heart is about to tear apart. This wretched feeling may be caused by a variety of circumstances. Perhaps their spouse or lover is out of town and they are overcome by longing. Or when they have expectations that their son will become a doctor and instead he is caught in a club with drugs and an unregistered firearm. Someone won the lottery but lost their ticket. In such circumstances, they will probably feel *hǔa jai thÊEp jà khàat*. They experience a feeling of despair that makes them feel heart-broken. As the following heart phrases suggest, the Thai language has a rich arsenal of heart expressions for the English language notion of sadness that comes from a broken heart.

Dry Heart

jai hÊEng   ใจแห้ง

Whether the metaphor for the state of a person's emotional condition is withered as in *jai hǎaw* or dry as in *jai hÊEng*, the effect is the same: They are feeling sad or unhappy. The feeling is less powerful than *jai hǎaw*. Both of these emotions are reflected in the way a person speaks about the condition of the heart—conditions which suggest non-wellness of the person who experiences them. Since the heart and mind are not divided as in English, these states of sadness and unhappiness affect thinking as well as feelings.

Sad Heart

hǔa jai rá thom   หัวใจระทม

This is another heart expression to describe one's broken heart condition. In this state, a person possesses a deep, profound sense of sadness. The word *rá thom* means sadness of the gravest kind. Perhaps it is the death of a parent or friend that causes this penetrating sense of sadness to envelop their heart and soul.

Sad Heart

ráaw jai   ร้าวใจ

Someone feels that another has chipped off a piece of their heart. If the heart is a crystal vase, it has a crack down the center. They can still use the vase. Just as they won't die in this state of being, they definitely feel what happened has caused them to feel loss and sadness. He or she is experiencing heartache. The person may have been away for a couple of months and their lover has established a new relationship with someone else.

Sad Heart

salòt jai   สลดใจ

When someone witnesses another's true misfortune in life, then they may feel *salòt jai*. This is sadness in the sense of empathy or sympathy for another's black luck or harm. One become sad in the heart about the misadventure suffered by another. He or she may have come upon a terrible automobile accident and witnessed the suffering of those injured.

A second situation for using *salòt jai* is to describe a major disappointment. The feeling may arise when someone who is close to one commits an act or says something which is disappointing. A child may be caught out in telling a lie and this disappoints his mother. The event in question is significant. It would not refer to a trivial disappointment. But what is trivial to one may be of profound significance to another. Take the case of a spouse who promised to attend an important social event, then changes his or her mind and refuses to go after all, and the resulting disappointment may cause the feeling of *salòt jai* to one person yet of trivial significance to another. On the other hand, some misfortunes are universally significant. If a newspaper reports a plane crash with all passengers dead, then most readers would experience a "sad heart." Another variation of this heart phrase is *anàat jai*.

Sad Heart

thúk jai   ทุกข์ใจ

This heart phrase is the classic expression of sadness. *thúk jai* is commonly used to express the daily, garden variety states of unhappiness in life. Someone who wakes up in the morning to find that their car has been broken into overnight and the radio has been stolen is likely to feel *thúk jai*. Or if someone is laid off or fired from their job, they would also use this expression (among others) to express their emotional state of being.

Shrivelled Heart

hǔa jai lîip   หัวใจลีบ

"Shrivelled heart" is a slang phrase to express the sense that someone has a broken heart. The use of the word *lîip* has a meaning similar to shrivelled. Alternatively, this heart phrase can be used to mean one suffers from heart disease. The metaphysical state of the heart must be distinguished from physical condition of the heart and this usually is evident from the context in which the phrase is used.

Sinking Heart

jai pÊEw   ใจแป้ว

When a person hears the bad news about a friend who has lost his wife, home, and job, and they experience their heart sinking in reaction to this news. They are feeling a mini-collapse inside their chest. The feeling is *jai pÊEw*. It is the empathy of feeling another's loss or pain as one's own. Or they may feel *jai pÊEw* if they find out the person they love is in love with someone else. Or when a woman discovers that her lover is married when she thought he was divorced, she will likely feel, among other emotional states, *jai pÊEw*.

Withered Heart

jai hěaw   ใจเหี่ยว

A person feels sad or dismayed about something or about what someone did or said, or with their own actions. Also, they may have witnessed a terrible event like a major injury or death of a child. The state of sadness expressed in *jai hěaw* is probably not too great or longlasting, although the immediate impact may be great at the time it is experienced. The sadness is a short-term jolt from which you will likely recover quickly. Perhaps one forgot to send a Father's Day card to their father and has realized their oversight. Or they may have overheard their secretary (someone whose opinion they value) telling another employee that the boss arrived at annual office party sporting an ugly necktie and bad haircut.

Sensitivity
Touchy Heart

nÓOy jai   น้อยใจ

nÓOy núea tàm jai   น้อยเนื้อต่ำใจ

nÓOy òk nÓOy jai   น้อยอกน้อยใจ

Those with a "touchy" heart are often of a certain personality type. Small things in daily life cause them anguish, easily disturb their mood. Such an individual is wounded by a disapproving glance as well as a thoughtless word. Criticism is something that is not well-tolerated by the "touchy heart". Should one suggest to the *nÓOy jai* person that he should stop smoking, he would take offense, cut off the conversation and sulk. The teenaged son or daughter who is asked to refrain from using the telephone or television, if they have a "touchy heart"—and most teenagers do—will feel slighted or hurt. There are those individuals, however, who remain sensitive to any hint of disapproval, limitation, restriction or criticism for a lifetime. These are the truly "touchy hearted" amongst us.

Shame

Abashed Heart

khŭay jai ขวยใจ
krà dàak jai กระดากใจ

This is one way of expressing a person's shame for having done the wrong thing at the wrong time. In their reaction to another, they have miscalculated their intention, morality and commitment. Perhaps a person has accused a servant of taking money but later they discover the missing sum in their desk drawer. The servant was blameless; the accuser has mistakenly attributed wrong conduct to the servant. In such circumstances that accuser might feel *khŭay jai.*

Shame Heart

rúu sùek lá aay jai รู้สึกละอายใจ

A person has done something wrong and feels ashamed for their actions. Many people may not admit they have ever felt "shame heart". This is a person's conscience talking through their heart. One might feel shame because they treated their spouse or child unfairly or without due consideration for their feelings. A wife requests that her husband goes with her to visit her mother for the Loy Krathong festival but he demands that she go with him to Singapore. Later, after the husband reflects on his actions and understands he acted selfishly, then he may feel *rúu sùek lá aay jai.* It is late at night and one comes across the scene of a road accident. There is no one else on the road and the person sees several injured people at the crash site. Rather than stopping to render assistance, he or she speeds up and drives past the site. Not long afterwards, they feel shame in their heart for failing to help.

Weariness
Aimlessness Heart

plÒOy jai   ปล่อยใจ

"Aimlessness Heart" applies to that momentary feeling arising in these two circumstances: (1) the feeling that there is nothing worth doing and (2) when one is doing something but it is boring or feels useless. In both instances, the person feels without a sense of direction or purpose. This feeling is lifted when the person feels a renewed sense of purpose or the bored feeling drifts away. Lek works in a factory where her job is to stuff baby corn into cans ten hours a day, six days a week. She feels bored with this work. Her mind drifts from the baby corn stuffing to a daydream about going out to see a film with her friends. Her act of daydreaming is *plÒOy jai*. Another person may be in her room after work with nothing to do. She may not necessarily be bored but the absence of any direction at that moment allows her mind to drift into a daydream about a new restaurant. Often one can see this emotional state in someone's eyes. They appear to be very far off, lost in their personal thoughts, and one may ask them what they are daydreaming about by reference to this heart phrase.

Bored Heart

rá aa jai   ระอาใจ

ìt năa rá aa jai   อิดหนาระอาใจ

The heart phrase is employed when one is fed up or bored with an activity or another person's behavior. A student may sit in his or her room reading an English language book for hours. But he or she does not understand the grammar rules and after hours of attempting to master the rules, becomes totally bored and throws the book at the wall. A small child may run around a shopping mall picking up items and the mother runs after the child, putting the items back. After a certain period, the mother will feel *rá aa jai*. Another example is listening to a friend repeat a story about a trek in Chiang Mai for the nineteenth time. The listener feels *rá aa jai*.

Disheartened Heart

rá hèa jai   ระเหี่ยใจ

This heart phrase of *rá hèa jai* refers to someone (and it may be you) who appears tired or bored. Occupying this state of boredom, the heart is disheartened. Rather feeling angry, they fall into a sluggish state of lethargy. One has heard the same song on the radio day after day; one rolls one's eyes, shakes one's head, enters a state of torpor, softly sighing. The person sharing another's room may ask if they are *rá hěa jai*. The underlying feeling of boredom can be caused by any number of factors. Such as, they have been locked up in their apartment for several weeks working or they are bored eating the same kind of pizza ten nights in a row.

Tired Heart

nùeay jai   เหนื่อยใจ

The feeling is one of being tired and discouraged. The underlying cause is likely to have been a breakdown of communication with another person. For example, someone has tried on many ocassions to express their point of view on a subject and to explain how important their view is, but each time the other person fails to understand them. Perhaps the feeling might arise when their spouse or lover fails to understand their intention. She or he may have made every effort to understand their point of view, but simply cannot comprehend the true meaning. For example, one person may place a high premium on being punctual but his or her friend, spouse, or lover is chronically late. They explain the importance of being on time. The explanation is listened to but never acted upon. At some point, they have the realization that she or he will never understand the value they attach to being on time, or that their sense of time is not understandable, then one is likely to feel *nùeay jai*.

Very Tired Heart

nùeay jai thÊEp khàat   เหนื่อยใจแทบขาด

One has experienced a long, hard Monday and feels bone-tired. Or it may be Wednesday morning and they have bags under one's eyes from a late Tuesday night. One knows that one needs a few more hours of sleep to function but, at the same time, one has an urgent appointment at the office. Instead, one forces themself to go into the office even though one feels exhausted physically and emotionally. When a secretary sees a person in this wasted condition, she may label him or her as *nùeay jai thÊEp khàat*.

Weary to Death Heart

ÒOn jai lǔea koen	อ่อนใจเหลือเกิน
ÒOn jìt ÒOn jai	อ่อนจิตอ่อนใจ
ÒOn òk ÒOn jai	อ่อนอกอ่อนใจ

When one's son refuses to give up his spot in the rock'n' roll band and resume his computer studies, and one has tried every known means to persuade him that good education is important for his future, yet one continues to fail in his or her efforts, then the parent will likely experience this feeling of fatigue. The sense of weariness comes from repeated attempts to change another's behavior or course of action and the failure of success despited repeated attempts.

Heart Talk
Compliments

Chapter 3

In the Thai language you learn to give and receive compliments by making references to the "heart". Bestowing a compliment opens up a rich source for "heart" metaphors. This chapter includes the standard "heart" phrases used in traditional social settings where compliments are exchanged between Thai speakers. In each case, an aspect of the person's character, personality, or attractiveness is the subject of the compliment.

The heart phrases—whether in the verb or noun form—are expressions of the speaker's own feeling, or a statement about the feelings of another. Heart compliment expressions range from *jai dii* ("good heart") to *nám jai* ("water heart"). In each case there is an approximate English translation of the Thai.

In mastering these phrases, notice which attributes of the heart are given expression: (i) the strong use of metaphor such as the eye or water; (ii) abstract virtues such as trust, bravery, merit, comfort, and boldness; (iii) physical features, such as broadness, softness, and size.

If you wish to pay a Thai speaker a compliment the chances are you will find an appropriate expression among these heart compliments. Some of the warmest Thai expressions are compliments about how a speaker feels about another person. A word of caution is in order. Do not overuse the heart compliments. Thais are sensitive and fully aware of those who attempt to use their language in order to falsely flatter them. If you have chosen a phrase that does not ring true to a Thai speaker, you may hear the return phrase—*pàak wäan* ปากหวาน—sweet mouth. This means you are sugar-coating your words and that you are not expressing genuine feelings. Your integrity is on the line when you pay a heart compliment especially with someone you have not known for a long period of time.

It is important to distinguish two general types of heart phrases in connection with giving or receiving compliments. One category is about flattery (given or received) while the other category is about genuine feelings about being impressed by another, state of affairs or thing.

Captivating Heart

nâa jàp jai　　น่าจับใจ

A good story or tale captivates the reader or listener. A girl writes a heart-felt article for Mother's Day about what a wonderful mother she has. The article is published in the newspaper. Those who read the story are impressed or captivated by the truth of the writer's emotions. Someone who relates in vivid detail his or her exploits in finding rare relics in the jungles of Burma, and in so doing, has the entire table captivated, listening to the story. The readers or listeners in the above examples would feel that the newspaper article and story about Burma were *nâa jàp jai.*

Eat Heart

kin jai　　กินใจ

kin jai comes from the feeling of being impressed with another person, an event, or object. What is impressive may speak volumes about the individual so impressed. A person may feel impressed with the story in a film, book, a display of fireworks, or the sporting skill of a world-class athlete. You have seen Casablanca fifteen times and still are taken in by Bogart's performance as Rick, the bar owner. You feel *kin jai* about "Rick".

Flatter Heart

phûut aw jai　　พูดเอาใจ

If someone say to you after you have given a compliment: *phûut aw jai,* it means they feel you are flattering them. The seriousness of the compliment or your true intentions in making the compliment are being questioned. You might hear this phrase after you have told someone who is fifty years old that he or she looks to be twenty-nine or you tell someone plain-looking that she is beautiful or he is handsome. *phûut aw jai* translates as an ulterior motive: you are appear to be speaking from your heart, but, in fact, your heart is false because you want something from the person who you are speaking with. You are saying what you believe the other person wishes to hear rather than saying what you believe to be true. It is another variation on *pàak wäan* or "sweet mouth".

Stamp Heart

prà tháp jai ประทับใจ

trueng taa trueng jai ตรึงตาตรึงใจ

If you want to compliment a Thai about Thailand you can say you feel *pràtháp jai* or impressed with Thai food, the beaches of Koh Sumui, the Grand Palace, or the ancient culture of art and dance. Many tourists, who return year after year to Thailand, feel a sense of *pràtháp jai* about the kindness and smiles found in abundance throughout the Kingdom. You may also experience this feeling about the devotion, kindness, courage or wisdom of another person. Such a person stands above the rank and file of humanity by being noble, selfless, or extraordinary in talent, temperment or accomplishment.

Compassion/Consideration

Catch Heart

jàp jai จับใจ

The phrase "catch heart" can also be translated as "arrest heart". Such a person can easily and effectively express their emotions, whatever they are feeling is evident. Fluency in communicating emotions means the communicator has the ability to catch or arrest the heart of another. Thus *jàp jai* is taking another heart into custody. But to catch another person's heart in any language is an art, not a science. It is that rare ability to touch another person on their emotional wavelength. When you can tune someone into that frequency in a persuasive fashion with your expression of feelings, the chances are you will capture their heart.

Comfort Heart

plÒOp jai ปลอบใจ

Someone you know is experiencing emotional pain or distress and you seek to give comfort. The comfort you offer comes from your heart, and the feeling of comforting another is *plÒOp jai*. You provide comfort to others through your heart by lending a sympathetic ear, giving them emotional support and guidance. The emphasis is on the helping aspect of dealing with a person who is suffering emotional pain or a setback. This heart phrase is often used in a similar way as *hěn jai*.

See Heart

hěn jai   เห็นใจ

hěn òk hěn jai   เห็นอกเห็นใจ

When you know someone who has suffered some personal misfortune or setback, and you go out of your way to do something considerate which shows your sympathy with their hurt, anguish or suffering. By your act of sympathy, you are "seeing" their pain with your heart and this feeling of compassion is *hěn jai*. Noi's wife has left him, and he is miserable. He is your friend and you invite him out to dinner in order to cheer him up. You feel sympathy for his plight and hope the dinner will take his mind off his troubles. A person who *hěn jai* another person will sympathize and help that person who has suffered an emotional trauma or upset. You give sympathy from your heart.

True Heart

jing jai   จริงใจ

The true hearted person is someone who expresses their true feelings of love, care or consideration. They do not hide their emotional state behind a veil of deceit. Such a person does not resort to using guile to obtain an advantage. If these things are true of you, then you possess *jing jai*. You have no time or patience for masks or deception in your words or behavior. People always know where they stand with you. Great value is placed on plain, straight speaking and actions. The reward for meeting this high standard is to be known as someone who has a true heart. True to others, true to themselves.

Confidence
Confident Heart

mân jai   มั่นใจ

The phrase conveys a certainty of feeling you have about another person. In the context of a personal relationship, this heart phrase ranks as a high compliment. When another person feels *mân jai* about you, that means feelings of distrust, suspicion, or doubt have disappeared. A feeling of great intimacy is required before this state of the heart is achieved. This *heart* phrase is frequently heard on Thai TV and in radio ads. The assumption is that product sales will increase through ads promising consumers that they will have a confident heart if they wear, display, eat, or drink an advertised product.

Firm Heart

jai nàk nÊEn ใจหนักแน่น

Some Thai women believe that it is important that their men have *jai nàk nÊEn*. The idea behind "firm heart" is the kind of personality that has an edge, a highly developed sense of personal confidence. Such a person stands out as being superior in knowledge and intellect, and ability to handle the matter at hand. Such a person is not easily taken in or deceived. There is the outward appearance of being in control and being on top of the situation.

Strong Heart

jai khêem khà ng ใจเข้มแข็ง

When someone believes strongly in themselves then they have *jai khêem khà ng*. If he or she is in the army and on the front line and they have been given the order to advance against the enemy, having a "strong heart" or *jai khêem khà ng* provides the confidence to face the danger. The heart phrase captures a feeling of strength and conviction in oneself. Without such confidence coming from the heart, a person is made timid and may lack the confidence to take those risks necessary to succeed.

Trust Heart

wáy jai ไว้ใจ
wáy waang jai ไว้วางใจ

You trust another with your heart. Whether the person you are relying on is your wife, child, employee, driver, or friend, this is a person who you trust with your secrets, your confidence, the information that is most important to you. To reach this stage of "trust heart" means that you have made a judgment about this person's loyalty and faithfulness. And you believe they will not let you down. When you give the "green light of trust" you are saying, in Thai, that you *wáy jai* that person. The central aspect of this heart phrase is, "My heart trusts you". Trust has a universal meaning in every language. The elements include truthfulness, not deceiving or betraying another, and believing and relying upon the honorable intentions of others.

Courage
Bold Heart

jai dèt   ใจเด็ด

This may be a compliment depending on the context. When you stand your ground, when you are fearless in the face of a threat or adversity, then you have *jai dèt*. Like the phrase *jai klâa*, this phrase is a comment on your personal attribute as one who can withstand panic in the face of fear. On the other hand, if you recklessly expose yourself to danger—for example, you walk out on Sukhumvit Road and expect traffic to stop for you to pass—you may be said to have *jai dèt*. The spin, in such circumstances, turns the compliment into something that is not necessarily a compliment: it translates that you are bold and stupid, a dangerous, if not fatal, combination.

Brave Heart

jai klâa   ใจกล้า
jai sĭng   ใจสิงห์

If you are the kind of person who does not show fear or is not afraid, and others sense this about you, then you may hear someone comment that you have *jai klâa*. This heart phrases defines a person's appetite for risk. A person who is not afraid of the uncertainty of a situation or the unknown consequences of an action has a "brave heart". Riding on the back of a motorcycle taxi through heavy Bangkok traffic is having a large dash of *jai klâa*. Helping someone who is being mugged on the street is having *jai klâa*. The threat may be less visible. For example, going unescorted to an ATM machine late at night might be another example of *jai klâa*. A woman, wearing several two-baht gold chains, walking alone on an unlit, isolated *soi* at two in the morning possesses *jai klâa*. An investor who buys shares on the SET as the market drops like an anchor has *jai klâa*. To ignore risk or danger and to proceed requires the possession of *jai klâa*.

Bully Heart

jai nák leeng   ใจนักเลง

The person (man or woman) with *jai nák leeng* fits the profile of a bully. Someone who pushes their weight around, seeking to enforce their authority over others. On occasion the bully may be on the side of the weak person and appear to be a hero. Other times, the bully may seek to intimidate others with threats of force or violence, causing them to be fearful.

Daring Heart

jai thǔeng   ใจถึง

This is alternative way to express the same sentiment as boldness as *jai dèt*. You rush to rescue a friend who is being assaulted by a couple of thugs. This requires you to possess a "daring heart".

Strong Heart

jai khOO nàk nÊEn   ใจคอหนักแน่น

The person with a "strong heart" is someone who rarely changes their mind. Another definition would be single-minded in pursuit of a goal. Someone who is determined to obtain a Master's degree in English Literature, who holds down a full-time job and studies until early into the morning each day would have a strong heart.

Generosity

Big Heart

jai yày   ใจใหญ่

The basic idea behind this expression is similar to *jai pâm*. You are the kind of person who takes your friend's children to a music lesson because their mother is ill and cannot make the journey. In performing this act of grace, you convey the sense of someone who acts without ever asking for payment or reward. You are *jai yày* when you act out of larger duty towards others. Others think of you as someone with a sense of responsibility for them as if they were part of your extended family.

If someone refers to you as *jai yày*, then you have done something to deserve the compliment of having a large heart. You might have adopted several orphans and paid to put them through school. Perhaps you volunteered your time working on a hot-line for troubled teenagers. You are *jai yày* when your heart has a large capacity for feeling sympathy with your fellow man. At the same time, some Thais might say there is a flaw in the nature of someone who is always doing or spending more than is normally expected.

Broad Heart

jai kwâang   ใจกว้าง

jai khOO kwâang khwǎang   ใจคอกว้างขวาง

You may be the kind of person who is generous and unselfish in your personal relationship. If so, then you qualify as having *jai kwâang*. Your actions and manner suggests to those around you, that you care about those who are less fortunate. The person who has *jai kwâang* is sensitive to the needs of others. You automatically pick up a bar bill or restaurant check, or you offer another person a lift in your car. When there is a fire in a slum, you send food, clothing, and building material to those who are suffering. You offer help or assistance as part of your daily routine, and if you do so long enough, you are bound to hear a Thai refer to you as having *jai kwâang*.

jai khOO kwâang khwäang is another variation of the noun *jai kwâang* and refers to the same kind of considerate, thoughtful person.

Generous Heart

jai too   ใจโต

nâa yày jai too   หน้าใหญ่ใจโต

nám jai an kwâang khwǎang   น้ำใจอันกว้างขวาง

jai tòoep   ใจเติบ

These four heart phrases are similar to the "merit heart" phrase *jai bun*. You have the qualities necessary to make you a generous person in your actions with others. Others who come in contact with you sense that you are not tight with your wallet, your affection, or your attention to the needs of others. You are generous with others. And those who are the object of this generosity sometimes respond by using this heart phrase.

Sporting Heart

jai pâm   ใจปั้ม

This is a positive or good quality in another person. Someone who spends money freely with others is *jai pâm*. Such a person often takes the form of the leader of the group. The one the others look to in making decisions or expressing opinions. Such a person establishes his position with small gestures. For example, when the check for the meal arrives at a table full of friends this person picks it up and proceeds to pay for it. It is more common for foreigners to ask for separate checks in a restaurant. Such a practice is the opposite of *jai pâm*.

Very Happy Heart

hǔa jai phOOng too   หัวใจพองโต

This emotional state of happiness occurs when someone receives a special gesture or gift at an unexpected time or place. It applies to the person giving as well as to the person on the receiving end. A parent will feel *hǔa jai phOOng too* when making a gift to their son or daughter as a result of seeing the surprise and happiness on their face. Another example would be if Lek does not expect her boyfriend to collect her from school or work, and expects to take a taxi to meet him for dinner. But, to Lek's suprise, the boyfriend arrives in his car and they drive to the restaurant together. Lek feels *hǔa jai phOOng too*.

Goodness

Good Heart

jai dii   ใจดี

jai dii is one heart compliment you want attached to you. One of the first complimentary phrases you may hear as a foreigner and indeed which is a compliment—is *khun jai dii* which translates, "You have a good heart." *jai dii* is a common response in Thai when you perform an unrequested act of kindness or assistance. The key is that the action your have taken was intended to help another be it financial or personal. Whatever the nature of the help, your action had not been requested but arose from the goodness of your heart. In the Thai social system, requesting something from another exposes you not only to rejection but is a basic violation of the *kreeng jai* (see Chapter 6)—or the consideration one owes to others in the social order. *jai karunaa* is a more polite, formal expression for *jai dii* and normally appears in written form.

An important part of this consideration is not to ask or request your superior, your elder, your employer for something directly. Through indirect means, the need or desire might be communicated, leaving the "higher" ranked person with full discretion whether to act or not to act. To act in favor of the person who wants but is constrained from asking is *jai dii*.

If a Thai speaker has done something unexpected, something beyond which you have asked, then it is appropriate to refer to that person as *jai dii*. Thai speakers, like most people, would like to have friends and associates they feel are *jai dii*.

Good Heart Fights the Tiger

jai dii sûu sǔea   ใจดีสู้เสือ

This heart phrase means that the person with a good heart can overcome an adversary who may be stronger. The adversary may be a wild animal, or it may be a madman or armed robber. The courage of the man with a good heart, it is felt, can prevail over evil. Thus when a police officer who, unarmed, risks his life to rescue a child from the arms of a madman who is holding a knife to the child's throat, and succeeds, then others may comment: the policeman felt *jai dii sûu sǔea.*

Good Heart, Ghosts Enters

jai dii phǐi khâw   ใจดีผีเข้า

A person with a really good heart, one who is always helpful and available to assist others may be taken advantage of in a society where *kreeng jai* inhibits the asking of favors. If it is known, however, that one can freely asks favors of another, that person may find himself or herself taken advantage of as people seek her or him out for assistance. Thus a heart that is too good and helpful finds that "ghosts" will enter it. In this case, the ghost is a metaphor for one who is released from the *kreeng jai* inhibitions (meaning there is no fear or rejection of criticism to risk) and who is asking the favor.

Honest Heart

sùt jarìt jai   สุจริตใจ

"Honest heart" is similar to *bOOrisùt jai.* The heart phrase indicates that although there has been a misunderstanding or something has gone wrong, the person had no bad intentions. Since blame often follows the assignment of bad motive or harmful intentions, to plead that one is *sùt jarìt jai* is to plead that the person is innocent. For example, a patron leaves the restaurant; the waitress flies out after him or her claiming they didn't pay the bill. But he or she thought their friend had paid it. They claim to be *sùt jarìt jai* and explain there has been a misunderstanding. No fraud or wrongdoing was intended. Whether the "honest heart" explanation is accepted is another matter. But with an accusation of dishonesty, the honest person may claim to be *sùt jarìt jai.*

Pure Heart

bOOrisùt jai   บริสุทธิ์ใจ

This phrase applies to the sort of person who has retained his or her childlike innocence into adult life. Such an individual has not become cynical or hardened by the bumps in the road of life. The essence of being a child—sincere, curious, trusting, loving a purity of feeling and perception—has survived through childhood and continues to exist and shape his or her view of the world. If these attributes are true of you, then you might hear a Thai speaker refer to you as having *bOOrisùt jai.*

Soft Heart

jai ÒOn   ใจอ่อน

You have a soft heart and go out of your way to help your friends, family, children—that makes you *jai ÒOn.* Such a person places his personal relationship higher than his self-interest. If you are *jai ÒOn* then you must be giving, respectful, and thoughtful in your relationships. And those relationships must mean a great deal to you. Unlike *jai dii,* which may apply to an isolated act of kindness, *jai ÒOn* is more the general pattern of behavior over a long period of time. There is also a negative side to possessing a soft heart. It can mean that such a person can easily be taken advantage of by others. That the soft hearted person is flawed by satisfying the needs of others without looking after his or her own needs. One wishes this heart status for one's spouse, boss, friends and associates. At the same time, in a tough, protracted negotiation for a joint venture, the person who is soft hearted may end up with terms that will be detrimental to them.

Kindness

Nurture Heart

thanŎOm jai   ถนอมใจ

One aspect of kindness is sparing the feelings of others. In the case of "nurture heart" that may require a person to tell a little white lie. In other words, telling someone what they want to hear rather than the reality or truth of a situation. For instance, it is Lek's birthday and her sister bakes her a birthday cake. Unfortunately the sister is a terrible cook and the cake is filled with all the wrong ingredients and no one, not even the *soi* dogs, would eat it. However, Lek puts on a good face in the presence of her sister and makes an effort to consume a small piece of the cake, smiling and telling her sister that it is wonderful. Lek has *thanŎOm jai* (and perhaps a case of heart burn as well).

Token of Appreciation Heart

sĭn nám jai   สินน้ำใจ

This is a slightly different phrasing of *nám jai* and is used in the same context and this is a quality a person has. The phrase carries the idea of remuneration—a gift or cash—which is given to another as a token of feeling for another. *sĭn* translates as money or property. For example, you may show your appreciation for an act of kindness or a display of loyalty by giving another person a hilltribe antique silver bracelet. Your secretary had a baby girl and you go to the hospital with flowers and a gift. These acts are a token of appreciation on your part.

True Heart

nám sǎy jai jing   น้ำใสใจจริง

The literal translation of this delightful phrase is clear water, true heart. When you hear these words uttered about yourself, it is likely that you have gone out of your way to help someone without any thought of payment or reward. You did what you did out of some genuine or true feeling of giving rather than as a commercial or mercenary act. For you the smile of gratitude is currency in which you are paid; and when you hear the words *nám sǎy jai jing* put yourself down as having received a million-dollar emotional pay day.

Water Heart

nám jai   น้ำใจ

When someone makes an effort to remember another person, or takes into account his or her feelings, for example by bestowing a small gift when invited to dinner or after returning from a trip abroad to an employee, staff, or servant, such a person is said to possess *nám jai*. Everyone likes to feel they are important, that they matter, and that others take them into consideration. In Thailand, one way of expressing your "water heart" is through a simple gesture of appreciation. Often "water heart" translates as acts of common courtesy. Giving up your seat on the bus for an elderly person, allowing the person with one or two items to go ahead of you at cashiers in the supermarket, or permitting another car to enter the traffic in front of you. "Water heart" doesn't take much effort. Inside such a heart is the understanding that such small gestures are the glue that holds society together, makes us all a little more human and decent, and reminds us there is something to admire in people who take into account other people have feelings. The way a person with a "water heart" treats another touches all of us.

Willing Heart

tem jai   เต็มใจ

tem òk tem jai   เต็มอกเต็มใจ

tem jai applies to a person who possesses the basic willingness to help others without any thought of receiving a reward or recognition of his or her acts. Such acts of kindness and friendship come from the good nature of a selfless person who is motivated by making the world a little bit better by lending a hand to others. You help others with a demonstration that you have willing heart—a heart which automatically goes out to provide support and comfort to another person who is in need.

Nobility

Merit Heart

jai bun   ใจบุญ

Good Heart

jai bun sǔn thaan   ใจบุญสุนทาน

Merit heart applies to the kind of person who rises at the crack of dawn and hands out food to monks. Or when you see someone in distress you try to comfort them. If you give money to a child beggar, then many Thais might think you are *jai bun*. Or someone is dying in hospital because they can't get a blood match, and you volunteer to donate your blood. By such actions, you are making merit. In Buddhism if you make merit in this life, you will be born to a better life next time around. This heart expression is an illustration of the relationship between Buddhism and the heart in a phrase that is intended as a high compliment.

Monk Heart

jai phrá   ใจพระ

You are the kind of person who is never angry and never hurts another's feelings, and that makes you *jai phrá*. The phrase refers to an ideal person who always takes into account the other people's feelings and needs before taking into account his or her own. Such a person has saintly qualities, and in a world of grasping, greed and self-interest; few such people exist out the of temples. Therefore, this is a rare heart phrase to use or to hear others use.

Noble Heart
khwaam sǔung sòng khǑOng jìt jai   ความสูงส่งของจิตใจ

The noble hearted person displays his or her acts of nobility in a number of ways. For instance, a person who goes to the ATM to withdraw funds from his account which has a balance of Baht 1,000 finds that the machine malfunctions and dispenses Baht 700,000 instead. Rather than pocketing the money and leaving, the "noble hearted" person returns the full amount to bank officials. The essence of this heart phrase is an act that would be against the immediate self-interest of the person performing it, but the act is in the larger interests of the community. Another example, is a person with very little money who gives away half of his lunch money to a friend who has no money for food. The act is more than a gesture of charity; it causes some loss or hardship to the person performing the noble deed.

Heart Talk
Condemnations

Chapter 4

Matters of the heart have a dark, stormy side. Chapter 7 is a brief introduction to the linquistic instruments of warfare. Such phrases are used when the heart is wounded or when seeking to wound the heart of another. In this chapter, the condemnations often have less emotive punch. That is not to say that to condemn another using one of these phrases may not inflict hurt feelings. Depending on the context in which such a heart phrase is used, they most certainly will. What are the condemnation heart phrases? These *jai* phrases are communicate to another either rejection, insults or criticism.

In any language it is always a question of degree whether a critical statement is intended to injure or is intended in jest. More than the phrase or words themselves come into play. Facial expression, gestures, the relationship of the parties, the context of the conversation are all relevant in assessing whether a heart phrase crosses the threshold of humor and becomes nasty. In extreme cases, it can be an oral declaraton of war. Using these phrases is a little like playing with fire: one can get burnt easily.

Often it may be too late to "take back" what is intended in jest as the person who is on the receiving end may have responded in a flash, with anger or with a weapon.

Using most of these phrases in a non-playful manner with a total stranger is the verbal equivalent of a midnight stroll through a minefield. You might get through without harm, but why run the risk in the first place?

Unless you are very experienced in flight or an expert on Thai culture and inter-personal relationships, it is better to find another phrase, or better another languages when you wish to resort to outright, direct criticism.

Remember that the Thai language has many expressions modified by heart that are critical of another's personality, reaction, or attitude. For example, laziness, and stupidity, or selfish, unsympathetic, careless actions by another are criticized in terms of that person's heart, or the feelings you experience if you are the subject of such a person's action.

While Thai speakers have a great capacity for humor and are masters of the fine art of joking, few people of any nationality could be reasonably expected to hear harsh, negative and judgmental phrases from another and maintain their smile. In many cases, such equivalent phrases would stay inside one's private thoughts, or at the very least they would be used out of the earshot of the person to whom the phrase is being applied.

Arrogance
Encourage Heart

dây jai   ได้ใจ

This heart phrase is a coin with two sides. One side is the positive aspect such as when a person is complimented or told he or she has done a job well, explained a solution to a problem with skill, or told he or she is attractive, smart, young and desirable. The result of such a compliment is for the person to feel *dây jai*. The other side of the coin, however, is negative. On the flip side of this heart phrase, is a person who communicates through action and words that he or she thinks he or she is better than someone else. There is a sense of arrogance about such a person. When people constantly tell another person that she or he possesses special talents, skills, or attractiveness, then she or he or she may develop a *dây jai* nature. "Encourage heart" means, in this context, conceit: and conceit is the brother (or sister) of selfishness.

Hubris Heart

lam phOOng jai   ลำพองใจ

húek hǒoem jai   ฮึกเหิมใจ

khúek khá nOOng jai   คึกคะนองใจ

These heart phrases apply to a person who behaves in an arrogant, impetuous or high spirited fashion. Someone who has obtained a measure of success, such as a financial windfall, and brags and/or displays his or her success in a boastful manner may hear one of these heart phrases used about them. The bragging and boasting is *lam phOOng jai*. The lucky winner of a lottery who goes boasts to his or her friends that he or she is rich but all the friends know that in reality the winnings were small and the person making the boast is not really rich at all. These heart phrases are a way of cutting through the artifice of display and boast to expose the truth.

Cowardliness

The main attribute of the coward is an action or inaction resulting from being afraid. There are degrees of fear, and the heart phrases gauge the relative lack of courage when a person is faced with the unknown or an obstacle in the pathway of life. Some may be afraid of their own shadow, or mistake a shadow for a ghost. Sometimes these heart phrases can be a taunt said with the intentioin of making someone do something that is otherwise foolhardly or reckless.

Timid Heart

jai sÒ   ใจเสาะ

This is a wonderfully expressive heart phrase, describing a number of different states of the classic fight or flight choice. Someone is walking down a strange *soi* and finds large, fierce dogs coming straight for them. They are likely to turn and run away. Not infrequently there is a report in the *Bangkok Post* or the *Nation* about a bus, truck, or for that matter just about any driver, who, having caused an accident, immediately flees the scene of the accident. For the native Thai speaker the person who is running way is *jai sÒ*.

Coward Heart

jai mây klâa   ใจไม่กล้า

jai khlàat   ใจขลาด

You don't have the courage of your convictions. Another usage is for a person who is afraid of new, uncertain situations. Perhaps a job has been offered but requires the person to relocate to another country. The person is fearful of leaving Thailand and turns down the offer. A colleague may say that he or she has a "coward heart". You talk about taking the two-month overland trek in Nepal, but at the last moment call it off. A week before the wedding you go into hiding because you are afraid of going through with the marriage. Or maybe someone is pushing you around in the office or at home, and rather than standing your ground, you give in, and acquire the reputation of being *jai mây klâa*—your heart is not brave.

Heart Carp

jai plaa siw   ใจปลาชิว

This adjective, like *jai sÒ* ("faint heart"), is a label attached to someone who is easily scared. Although in the case of *jai plaa siw* your cowardice makes you comparable to a frightened carp. The carp is thought to be easily frightened, a cowardly fish. So to be placed heartwise in the same league with a carp is far from a compliment, though it can be used in jest amongst close friends. In general, heart carp refers to a person who lacks the courage to stand up to another person or face danger; a person who feels overwhelmed and incapable of dealing with a situation or problem. The boss demands that you work over the weekend and you are afraid to tell him that it is your son's birthday and you are commited to taking the family on an outing. In such a case, your wife might refer to you as *jai plaa siw*.

Deception

Borrow Another's Nose to Breathe Heart

yuuem jamùuk khon ùuen hǎay jai   ยืมจมูกคนอื่นหายใจ

This the heart of a plagilarist. The deception is in the metaphor: another's nose is borrowed to breathe. Though, unlike the conman who has *nâa sûue jai khót* (see below), in this instant, the borrower may or may not use the mask of respectability to get his or her way. A person with such a heart is forever "borrowing" the labors, and/or goods of others. A person who pays another to write their examination or thesis to graduate from university has *yuuem jamùuk khon ùuen häay jai*. Also the neighbor or friend who is constantly borrowing tools, software, books, car and money is said to have such a heart.

Deceiving Heart

nâa sûue jai khót   หน้าซื่อใจคด

A heart phrase that sounds like the title of a country and western song. The person with *nâa sûue jai khót* wears a mask of deception. Normally the mask presented to others suggests that the person wearing it is good, honourable, decent and reliable, when, in fact, the person is seeking to cheat or take advantage of another. For instance, a person who is well-dressed and spoken stops a tourist who has been in Thailand for only three days and strikes up a friendly conversation. The tourist immediately trusts and likes the new friend who suggests they visit a jewelry shop. The con artist offers to take the tourist to this special shop where he or she will be given the chance to buy world class gems that the tourist is told can be resold in her or his country for a three hundred fold profit. In fact, the gems are of little value and the tourist will lose his or her money. This classic street scam is carried off by individuals with a "deceiving heart".

False Promise Heart
khÓ kà laa hây mǎa dii jai   เคาะกะลาให้หมาดีใจ

    The literal translation is giving the top half of a coconut shell to the dog, makes the dog happy. Someone makes a promise to do or give something to another but when the time arrives for performance, the promise maker does not deliver. The promise was false. This is a good heart phrase to remember when dealing with a company, an individual or a government officer. The person across the desk promises with a smiling face and all the assurance in the world that he or she will guarantee to have your phone installed, your computer repaired, your newspaper delivered to your new address or your application for a permit or licence processed not later than Friday morning. When Friday morning rolls around, however, these promises are not kept. Such a person possesses a "false promise heart".

Thieving Heart
muue way jai rew   มือไวใจเร็ว

    The person with a "thieving heart" has a quick hand, quick heart. One example would be a pick-pocket on a bus or in a busy shopping mall. The concept is the ability to take away something quickly without the owner of the property being aware of the taking. The heart phrase can also apply to someone who takes advantage of another with great speed and dexterity. For instance, Vinai is Lek's boss at the office and every time he walks past her desk, he quickly touches her shoulder or hair and then walks away before she has time to react.

Devils

Devil Heart
maan hǔa jai   มารหัวใจ

    The person with a "devil heart" is someone who destroys the love existing between people. This is the classic soap opera love triangle where a couple, husband and wife or boyfriend and girlfriend, find their counterpart in the relationship has entered into a loving, caring relationship with a third person. The effect is to alienate the affections of the deceived person. The outsider to the relationship who knowingly intervenes to cause the break-up of an existing relationship is *maan hŭa jai.*

Losers

The loser is the person easily manipulated. Someone who is sluggish and willing to be led down the garden path. Through innocence or lack of intelligence, such a person is not on guard that others may seek to take advantage.

Easily Influenced Heart

jai baw   ใจเบา

This is a heart phrase for a stupid person. The notion is someone who will trust just about anything you tell him. The moon is made of green cheese and inter-city *klongs* are suitable for bathing and drinking water. If you trust this easily then your actions are *jai baw.* This is Thai for actions that denote a sucker, someone easily taken in and led by another often against that person's best interest.

Passive Heart

jai chùeay   ใจเฉื่อย

This is automatic pilot mode, sluggish, slowed down into slow motion. Nothing much is going on inside a person, around that person except for the flicker of life on hold. It is a non-reflective mental state of being. If you are being lazy, hanging around the house or idling in a shopping center, a restaurant or a bar, doing nothing, staring off into the middle-distance, then someone may ask what you are doing. And your reply is likely to be wrapped up with being *jai chùueay.* This is a state of perfect idleness and, depending on your frame of mind and values, is either bad or good. If one returns to one's home country, then one may be only well-suited for a career of unemployment and welfare cheques, assuming such cheques continue to exist.

Intractable Heart

lǔea jai   เหลือใจ

The person who is *lǔea jai* will not accept no for an answer. She or he will continue to persist long after it become clear that the other person considers them a nuisance. The telephone sales person is a good example of someone who is *lǔea jai*. Such a person will continue to phone and attempt to sell a product or service even though the person indicates their lack of interest. Yet the sales person continues with her or his pitch. In the presence of someone who is *lǔuea jai* a person will be tested as to their ability to remain calm and cool in their heart.

Selfishness

Resources such as time and money are scarce. There is competition for what is available. In the midst of such competition some people are more generous and giving than others. Those individuals who in the pursuit of their happiness ignore the happiness or interest of others might be rightly called selfish. The heart phrases reflect a preoccupied or self-centered state of being. There are a number of *Heart Talk* phrases which suggest that in Thailand, selfishness is a highly personal emotional offence.

Diamond Heart

jai phéet   ใจเพชร

This heart phrase is sometimes used to describe a hardhearted person. A mother, for example, who abandons her infant is *jai phéet*. The father who disinherits his son because he wishes to study painting. The husband who neglects his wife's medical needs and fails to buy the medicine required to restore her health. Such a person suffers from the absence of any warmth or personal feeling about those who are the natural objects of such feelings.

Mean Heart

jai khÊEp   ใจแคบ

jai khOO kháp khÊEp   ใจคอคับแคบ

This is another expression of feelings to convey to others that one's action is or has been selfish. The "mean heart" or *jai khÊEp* person can't imagine anyone else in the world is more important or has needs more important than their own. Such a person thinks solely of his or her own pleasure or desire. If you expect the person with *jai khÊEp* to take you into account or consider your feelings or the impact of his or her actions on you, then you will be in for disappointment. For example, a friend is in need. Perhaps she or he is out of money to buy a bus ticket upcountry to visit an ailing mother, and rather than offer the money, the friend refuses. Such a person lacks *nám jai* or "water heart", and is someone with a mean spirit. Also, this kind of person is unable or unwilling to do those small gestures to help others even though the cost of doing so is very small.

No Notice Heart

mây aw jai sày   ไม่เอาใจใส่

This heart phrase broadcasts an all-points-bad news bulletin. The person who ignores you, pays no attention to you, gives you the signal she or he wants nothing to do with you is sending a message, the rough translation of which is: you don't exist in her or his eyes, heart or life. And this message of neglect and disinterest spins out from the heart: *mây aw jai sày*. It is acting as if another person is invisible.

Preoccupied Heart

jai mòk mûn   ใจหมกมุ่น

To possess an occupied heart is an indication of a person who is obsessed or compulsive in his or her actions. The woman in the movie *Fatal Attraction* had *jai mòk mûn*. Such a person becomes totally involved in his or her work project. Or they are obsessed with their lover like in the movie *Fatal Attraction*. They can't or don't want to eat or sleep. The "self" absorption is the key attribute. Such a heart is fully occupied and everything but that thing or person is squeezed out of their line of vision.

Selfish Heart

aw jai tua eeng   เอาใจตัวเอง

A person who acts in a selfish fashion may hear someone say that he is *aw jai tua eeng*. Such a person puts his or her desires and needs first and does not act with consideration towards others around them. The infractions may range from minor ones such as a midnight raid on the fridge where he or she eats the last piece of cake and drinks the last cola to the more serious incidents such as using the rent money for gambling or to buy a new watch.

Self-centered Heart

aw tâE jai ton   เอาแต่ใจตน

This heart phrase applies to the person who believes that the world revolves around their wishes, desires and dreams. Such a person may not be sensitive to the needs or desires of others. For instance, Lek loves Italian food. She always insists that her friends go to an Italian restaurant even though her friends would be more than happy to dine at a Thai restuarant. Lek would be terribly upset with her friends if they criticised her choice of restaurant or, even worse, refused to accompany her to restaurant. Another example is Vinai is the boss of a small factory. He sets high production requirements for his employees. One employee named Noi asks for a one-day leave of absence to attend the wedding of a friend who is getting married upcountry. The boss refuses on the grounds that without Noi, who is a top worker, his production schedule will not be met. The boss in Noi's eyes is *aw tâE jai ton*.

Mad Dogs, Killers and Ex-lovers

You may come across the cruel, the bad, and the hard people in all walks of life, and when you do, then in this section you are likely to discover a *heart* phrase to precisely describe such a person. Normally this kind of heart phrase would be used about a person in his or her absence. Using one of these heart phrases in a serious, angry manner may well result in a confrontation. One of the cultural rules in Thailand is to avoid confrontation with others. Thus when you hear such a phrase being used by Thai speakers it is usually spoken in a smiling, non-confrontational manner.

Bad Heart

jai chûa   ใจชั่ว

This is a Heart Talk adjective to be used with caution. It means you are attacking another person as a wicked, evil or mean individual. *chûa* is a grave insult in the Thai language. Depending on the context, *jai chûa* can easily become a call for confrontation and battle. *chûa* falls within the category of a curse. It ranks on the top ten list of Thai heart phrases which, when uttered to the wrong person at the wrong time, may earn you a trip to a local hospital.

Black Heart

jai dam   ใจดำ

This phrase is criticism hurled at you in circumstances where you fully understand another person's problem or setback and yet, despite your knowledge of the urgent need for help, you turn your back and walk away. A Thai friend requests a loan to pay for the hospital expense of her mother and you refuse even though you could easily afford making the loan. The friend may retort that you have a "black heart". The best English word to express the kind of person who bears the label *jai dam* is pitiless. The person without pity does not have empathy for the hardships and travails endured by others.

Cruel Heart

jai ráay   ใจร้าย

This is a commonly used heart phrase which covers conduct ranging from the stupid to the morally repugnant. At one end of the scale, a person may have made a stupid, silly mistake; he or she may have not taken into account another's feelings or desires. Normally, however, *jai ráay* is used for a person who has acted with cruel disregard for others. This kind of person might sell their own daughter into prostitution. Or she might be the kind of mother who throws out her daughter into the street because of a minor argument. The phrase applies to those in the hotel business who lock all fire escape doors to prevent guest from skipping out on their bill even though they know when a fire starts many people may die. Such people are *jai ráay*.

Hard Heart

jai khà ng   ใจแข็ง

Opinions differ on whether you have cursed or complimented another when using this phrase. It is a quality attached to the nature of a person. It can be good or bad depending on the circumstances presented. For example, if an external enemy is attacking your city you want soldiers who can fight the battle and defend the city. Thus *jai khà ng* is a good quality in a warrior. For a number of Thais, however, the phrase has a definite negative implication: You aren't the kind of person even your mother would like to admit knowing. There is an element of being self-centered, selfish, and even a slightly cruel spin to a person who is *jai khà ng*. Appeals made by others to your kindness, decency, or understanding roll off you emotionally like water off the back of a duck. You aren't moved emotionally by such requests, consider them irrelevant and unimportant in a life where it is dog-eat-dog.

Ruthless Heart

jai máy sây rá kam   ใจไม้ไส้ระกำ

Such a person must have a brutal, nasty, hard heart for someone to say he or she is *jai máy sây rá kam*. This heart phrase is a strong linguistic condemnation. The Thai speaker reserves such a phrase for a child killer, or other heavy criminal elements who intentionally cause pain or harm to other people and appear to suffer no feelings of remorse or guilt. The serial killer and the sadist fall within this category.

Tasteless Heart

jai jùuet   ใจจืด

jai jùuet combines heart with a Thai word—*jùuet*—which is often used to describe the tastelessness or blandness of food. The Thais pride themselves on spiced sauces, soups, and food. A bland dish is often pushed away uneaten. In matters of the heart, if you hear someone referring to you as *jai jùuet* your fate may be the same as the bland food—you will be left untouched and those around you will move around. The reason is others perceive that you have no feelings. It is as if on your emotional menu the main course of sympathy was left off. And without a steady diet of sympathy, life, like tasteless food, is a meal you might wish to forgo.

The Troubled

Those who are troubled in their heart and souls have a number of heart phrases to describe their condition or, as is more likely the case, to have their "troubled" heart described to them by others. There are appropriate heart phrases for the spoilt, careless, unfeeling, rude people who enter into your life. These are negative qualities and reflect the perceived defects in the hearts of others.

Careless Heart

cha lâa jai   ชะล่าใจ

This is a popular heart expression. When you tell several women you love them, promise them marriage or gold chains, and then disappear without saying goodbye, then you will be thought of as acting with a "careless heart". You act *cha lâa jai* when your tongue creates intentions which you cannot or will not act upon when the time for action comes. You are in love with the words of the heart; but short on the action needed to made the words reality.

Coarse/Rough Heart

jai krà dâang   ใจกระด้าง

A person may feel the absence of love for another, and if the other person is indeed in love, she or he, experiencing this vacuum of feeling in the other will experience *jai krà dâang*. The person on the receiving end of the "coarse/rough heart" label is likely to be someone who withholds emotional involvement. This may be evidence of a hardhearted person. Whatever one says or does, don't expect to move or touch such a person emotionally.

Hold Your Breath Until You Die Heart

klân jai taay   กลั้นใจตาย

When a person experiences a serious reversal of fortune or tragic events enter their life, they may feel hopeless and wish to die. It as if they wish to hold their breath and exit this veil of tears. When a couple breaks up, one person may be so distraught at the loss of the relationship that he or she wishes to hold his or her breath until they die. In Thailand, like in most countries, this is a fairly difficult threat to carry out. The second sense of the heart phrase is when someone is spoiled and wishes to have their way. A small child might use this expression with his or her mother because the mother refuses the child's request to buy the latest computer software game.

Rueful Heart

sĕa jai phaay lăng   เสียใจภายหลัง

You were given a warning not to buy (or sell) those shares on the stock market. But you thought you would make a killing. Instead you lost your entire investment. You remember the warning afterwards and the feeling that gives you is *sĭa jai phaay läng*—that sick feeling in the gut that you were stupid not to listen when you had the chance to do so. *sĭa jai phaay läng* is the feeling of knowing you did wrong, and applying self-criticism to your actions. You don't need anyone to point out you were a fool. You know it and feel it yourself.

Small Heart

jai nÓOy   ใจน้อย

jai nÓOy is a common expression heard among Thai speakers to describe a person who is on edge, touchy, or peevish. No matter what you say or do for someone who is *jai nÓOy,* it will never be sufficient, good enough, or right. This person will always find an excuse to complain, and nothing will be good enough for them. You approach such a person with caution because their chronic touchiness makes others around them uncertain and nervous and, ultimately, frustrated and angry. This small-hearted person is cranky and emotionally hovers near the boundary of a bad mood.

Spoilt Heart

jai tâEk   ใจแตก

Let Go of the Body, Let Go of the Heart

plÒOy tua plÒOy jai   ปล่อยตัวปล่อยใจ

One might use these two heart phrases to describe the actions of certain teenagers or anyone who lacks judgment. Such a person cannot distinguish between good and bad, or right and wrong. They have many friends who can lead them down the wrong path. They don't trust their parents. This is the equivalent of teenage rebellion—the James Dean syndrome. Unfortunately, these actions are not confined to those in their teens.

Heart Talk
in Relationships

Chapter 5

Understanding and correctly using heart phrases is essential in order to express feelings people experience in their relationships. Feelings of trust, joy, pain, desire, deception, doubt, and certainty are some of the themes found in many of the seventy-seven heart phrases contained in this chapter. A few of the phrases may be used to express feeling in circumstances other than a personal relationships such as *nÊE jai* ("sure heart") and *tuean jai* ("remind heart").

The personal relationship may be between: (i) husband and wife, (ii) boyfriend and girlfriend; (iii) parent and child; (iv) friends. Within the confines of such relationships, the Thai language allows the speaker to express his or her feelings of sorrow, pain, happiness, tenderness, trust, loyalty, and forgiveness.

Heart phrases also provide a rich vocabulary for lovers and friends to register the full scale of their feelings—from fury to tenderness. As you study the heart phrases you will better appreciate the universal emotional preoccupations embedded in the fabric of most relationships. What makes Thai heart phrases special is the wide range of feelings that we might associate with the feelings found in a love relationship.

The Thai language arguably has the largest number of heart phrases in any language. Each is rich in texture and nuance, allowing the speaker to express with precision his or her feelings within most relationships. The heart phrases, for purposes of convenience, have been divided into a thirteen general categories. The emotional landscape in a relationship draws those involved into a variety of mental conditions ranging from sadness to joy. Among Thai speakers, the art of learning and using these heart phrases is to discover a safe passage through the emotional minefields of a relationship.

There are a variety of heart phrases to articulate feelings of betrayal, dishonesty, deception, and disloyalty. Someone in the relationship has breached the bond of trust and acted out of self-interest, in a selfish fashion and often to the detriment of the other who has given their trust. These heart phrases refer to situations such as the workplace, the club house, and inside the family. In an intimate personal relationship, the partners expect to receive and to give loyalty and to be faithful. This ideal does not always prevail in reality. The man who loves two women, or the woman who loves two men is not *jai deaw* "one heart". When loyalty or faithfulness are questioned or disappear, the following phrases often come into play. Some of the heart phrases are condemnations of the person who has "many hearts".

Alarm Heart

tùuen tra nòk tòk jai   (ตื่น)ตระหนกตกใจ

Something unexpected crosses your path and the experience of the event is to send alarm bells ringing. The possible sources of alarm are multiple. You may switch on the news and find the outbreak of war, earthquake, floods, or other acts of nature are near your doorstep. You may be out for a late night walk and a mugger takes your wallet. You may be driving your car and come across a serious accident. In each of these cases the experience is the cause of emotional alarm. These are a few illustrations of circumstances which are likely cause feelings of alarm or *tùuen tra nòk tòk jai*.

Betray Heart

aw jai ÒOk hàang   เอาใจออกห่าง

A person walks into a crowded room with his lover and see the most beautiful woman he has ever laid eyes on crossing the room and giving him a seductive smile. Instead of moving on, ignorning this opportunity, he abandons his lover and escapes into the night with this beautiful stranger. The lover left behind is likely to feel despondent for having been involved with a man who is *aw jai ÒOk hàang*. In the underworld of gangsters, the heart phrase applies to a gang member who is disloyal to the gang, giving evidence to the police. In circumstances of double-dealing, the person who betrays another is rightly labelled as possessing a "betraying heart".

Crooked Heart

jai khót   ใจคด

The essence of a crook is someone who can not be fully trusted. They live outside the bounds of rules that most people abide by and believe are important. A man or woman who is disloyal to his partner is, in many ways, also placing themself outside of the normal expectations of what is permissible in a relationship. The nature of such a person, a relationship "outlaw", is *jai khót*. This translates as a person with some serious emotional breakage, damage that has never been repaired. The "crooked heart" is deceiving the other about his or her true feelings. For example, when the husband is away on the business trip the wife is out with another man, and when the husband returns she says that she stayed at home missing her lover. She is *jai khót*.

Doubting Heart

khlEEng jai   แคลงใจ

Mistrusting Heart

krìng jai   กริ่งใจ

These two heart phrases occur more frequently in written Thai. Occasionally when spoken, it appears when there is a question of breach of trust. Usually another person is the object of distrust or mistrust because of his or her actions or spoken words. It is similar in this way to *mây wáy jai*, which translates as "I do not trust you," or "I have doubts about you."

Easy Heart

jai ngâay   ใจง่าย

The "easy heart" applies to a man or woman who is promiscuous. The "easy hearted" person goes out with many different partners and sheds them like an old shirt. Such a person does not really connect emotionally with any partner. A man or woman such as this has a large appetite for diversity but no real, true feelings beyond the ones experienced in the moment. *jai ngâay* has a wider meaning: A person who is easily convinced or influenced by others; someone who has little capacity to reflect about a course of action and finds it easier to follow the lead of another.

Eye Far, Heart Far

klay taa klay jai ไกลตาไกลใจ

If you stay away from Thailand (or any place, for that matter) too long, those you have developed a relationship with and have been left behind are likely, over time, to start to forget about you. Memories about others fade quickly. So if you are far from another's eye, then her/his heart may travel away from you as well. The phrase is like the English usage: "out of sight, out of mind". In the Thai phrase *klay taa klay jai* it is the heart and not the mind that is far away.

Fickle Heart

jai loo lee ใจโลเล

A person with a "fickle heart" can not make up their mind about a relationship, job, shopping or the brand of toothpaste they want to use. She loves you tonight but tomorrow is another day, and she might have changed her mind overnight. There is an element of lack of commitment or an inability to make a decision and to keep steadfast with the outcome of what has been decided.

Heart with Many Rooms

jai mii lǎay hÔOng ใจมีหลายห้อง

The heart phrase is another description for someone who attempts to juggle several lovers or wives at the same time. It usually refers to a man who has several simultaneous relationships. Sometimes the phrase is used by a man to explain how he can rationalize having several ongoing relationships. The context of usage varies from a serious condemnation of a man to light repartee between friends. In most cases the phrase covers the same conduct as *lǎay jai*.

Many Hearts

lǎay jai หลายใจ

This heart phrase generally has two separate meanings. First, a "many hearted" person describes a character or personality who has many interests. For example, someone who loves tennis, skiing, and basketball. The second meaning refers to the character of a man who cares for many women. Such behaviour is significantly beyond the bounds of related heart phrases as "outside heart" and "second heart." A person who is *lǎay jai* cannot be faithful to one person. To be called *lǎay jai* in the second meaning is a clear message that someone has been written off as faithless, unreliable. Someone no one wishes to get deeply involved with.

Outside Heart

nÔOk jai   นอกใจ

Where the husband or wife has a relationship with another outside of the marriage or committed relationship. His or her action is *nÔOk jai*. The man with a minor wife, mistress or girlfriend exhibits classic *nÔOk jai* behaviour. Like the phrase *sŎOng jai* or "two hearts," the heart phrase is an emotional condemnation by those who view such behavior in negative terms. It also an explanation of how one person feels in a personal relationship where his or her loyalties are divided between two partners.

Pierce the eye, Pierce the Heart

tam taa tam jai   ตำตาตำใจ

Cut the Eye, Cut the Heart

bàat taa bàat jai   บาดตาบาดใจ

The essence of *tam taa tam jai* and *bàat taa bàat jai* is that the person who has been betrayed is a witness to the act of betrayal. Thus the act of disloyalty pierces the eye and also pierces the heart. The emotions registered would include loathing, anger and shock. The man who observes his sister-in-law stealing money from his brother's wallet, believing she is alone and unobserved. The child who is walking in a shopping mall and sees his father walking arm and arm with another woman who turns out to be the father's minor wife. Seeing his or her father in these circumstances would *tam taa tam jai* or *bàat taa bàat jai* the child.

Shared Heart

pan jai   ปันใจ

When a man has a major wife and continues to love and support her and at the same time has a minor wife whom he also loves and supports, it is said his heart is "shared" between the two women. The heart phrase can also apply to a woman who has two husbands, or one husband and a woman lover. This slang expression is taken from a Thai song.

Stabbed Heart

thîm thEEng jai   ทิ่มแทงใจ

The essence of the heart phrase is someone has been stabbed by the betrayal of a beloved. In this case, the betrayal occurs outside of the line of vision; that is, the person does not actually witness the act of betrayal but discovers it later. For instance, the boyfriend arrives back in Bangkok after six months abroad and discovers that his girlfriend has sold the five baht gold chain and diamong ring he bought for her. To add insult to injury, he discovers that she has used the money to buy her secret boyfriend, Somchai, a motorcycle. The acts of selling the jewelry and buying the motorcycle for the secret boyfriend would *thîm thEEng jai* her returning boyfriend.

Suspecting Heart

rá wEEng jai   ระแวงใจ

A wary heart is one with warning signals flashing. Something has gone emotionally wrong. The "suspecting heart" has doubts about the loyalty of another. For instance, a man arrives home at two in the morning with lipstick on his collar and his wife discovers the evidence; she will likely feel *rá wEEng jai* that he has been with another woman. The warning bell goes and she becomes wary about his explanation of having been delayed by the traffic on Sukhumvit Road.

Two Hearts

sǑOng jai   สองใจ

One person who loves two or more partners at the same time has *sǑOng jai*. The idea of loving more than one partner is translated into a person who possesses two hearts. This overcomes the obvious difficulty of cutting up a single heart for use with two lovers. Such a two-hearted person is frequently the subject of Thai TV soap operas, films, and books. In many such stories the battle is between a husband and his relationships (and divided loyalties) with a major and a minor wife.

Bluntness
Blunt Heart

thEEng jai dam   แทงใจดำ

The essence of *thEEg jai dam* is direct, straight talking. Bluntness of expression without necessarily taking into account the impact on the feelings of the other person. Normally, this is a negative characteristic. For example, someone who has just broken up with their spouse is seated next to a person who insists on bring up the subject at a restaurant with lots of other people at the table. The person who has gone through the painful break-up is trying to forget his or her personal problems but his friend is insistent on dragging out all the details of the divorce. The "blunt" person is speaking *thEEng jai dam.*

Character Traits

The character traits applying to people in a relationship can be (and often are) very different. There is a convenient method for conveying the essence of another person by use of the following heart phrases. It is important to remember these are merely illustrative of a vast number of potential character traits possessed by friends, lovers, colleagues and others with whom one has formed a relationship.

The examples are for a woman who has an innocent nature, a man who has a cruel nature and a child who is confused. As these heart phrases illustrate, the Thai language allows the speaker to exercise his or her own judgement as to the personality characteristics of others.

Bad Mouth, Good Heart

pàak ráay jai dii   ปากร้ายใจดี

Someone who uses cutting or insulting language (such as the vernacular of the fish market vendor) may have a heart of gold inside. The roughness or crudity of expression may not necessarily mean the speaker has a bad heart. For instance, in the Thai language there are crude ways to refer to oneself and others: *kuu* as oneself and *meung* as another. This is "gangster" talk. The person using such crude language may have a good heart and help people in the community by donating time and money. This heart phrase is a perceptive insight into the willingness of Thai speakers to forgive rough or crude language so long as the speaker is of good heart.

Child with Confused Heart

      hǔa jai dèk khon níi sàp sǒn   หัวใจเด็กคนนี้สับสน

The literal translation is: This child is confused. The confusion may be a temporary or permanent state. And as explained above, the state of confusion is not limited to childhood or to gender.

Man with a Cruel Heart

      hǔa jai phûu chaay khon níi hòot hêam   หัวใจผู้ชายคนนี้โหดเหี้ยม

The speaker assesses the man in question as someone who has a cruel or mean nature. Unlike the above heart phrase, it is unlikely to be used in the presence of the man who is being judged in this fashion. If so used, then it might well lead to a personal conflict. Also, there is no reason why a woman cannot have a cruel heart and a man an innocent heart. The use of the heart phrases here are not gender dependent but are reflections of the personal opinion of others on the characteristics of the person being judged.

Woman with Innocent Heart

      hǔa jai phûu yǐng khon níi bOOrisùt   หัวใจผู้หญิงคนนี้บริสุทธ์

The speaker assesses the woman in question as someone who has an innocent nature. Her heart is by definition pure. The literal translation is: This woman's heart is innocent and pure.

Condition

Condition of the Heart

      saphâap jìt jai   สภาพจิตใจ

This heart phrase is used to explain one's emotional state of being at the moment or describing such state in the past. One may feel a variety of emotions, including the feeling of being dejected, depressed, or sad; or one may feel happy, content, joyful. The communication of the "condition of the heart" may be made through words, gestures or acts of the person wishing to describe his or her emotional state of being. The employer or teacher, for instance, who is an expert in "reading" the "condition of the heart" of his or her employees or students will be able to provide them with appropriate comfort in times of need and to celebrate with them during times of joy.

Effort
Maximum Effort Heart

jai tem rÓOy   ใจเต็มร้อย

A person who possesses a "maximum effort heart" gives their full energy, concentration and spirit to an activity, friendship or romantic relationship. Such a person is completely committed to his or her efforts on making the activity, friendship, or romance a success. Such a person makes a very good employee, student, friend, lover or team-mate.

Fear
Afraid Heart

wàn jai   หวั่นใจ

phrân jai   พรั่นใจ

The phrase translates as fear of taking an emotional risk with another. Something holds the other person back emotionally. What causes fear in such circumstances depends on upbringing, life experience (good and bad), and personality. Some hearts bond more easily than others. Thus few generalization hold true in describing the class "afraid heart". Yet, one can be certain that a person feels 100% *wàn jai* if he/she suspects another person seeking a relationship is *läay jai*. Such a person is afraid of exposing their heart when it is certain to be broken. He or she will hold back until the bond can be made with a sense of trust and commitment.

Fear of Retribution Heart

wua sǎn lǎng khàat hěn kaa bin phàat kÔ tòk jai

วัวสันหลังขาด เห็นกาบินผาดก็ตกใจ

The literal translation is "the cow's spine is torn out, see the crow fly past quickly with a frightened heart." The essence, as the heart phrase suggests, is dread of retribution. Someone has done something wrong and consequently feels that the person who he or she harmed will seek justice for wrong suffered. The harm may have been a crime. The heart phrase covers other activities which stop short of criminal acts. For instance, an employee may have lied to his or her boss about the loss of an important contract, and a co-worker who knows the truth of the situation, exposes the lie to the boss. As a result the liar is *wua sǎn lǎng khàat hěn kaa bin phàat kÔ tòk jai* loses his or her job.

Fearful Heart

rá thúek jai   ระทึกใจ

Faced with a sudden flash of fear one feels *rá thúek jai*. If you are walking down a jungle path and meet a tiger, a "fearful heart" will no doubt be pounding in your chest. The same applies someone who is trying to cross Sukhumvit or Silom Roads or watching a horror film where the monster jumps out and makes a grab for the hero may cause a collective feeling of "fearful heart" in the audience.

Scared Heart

sǎw jai   เสียวใจ

This heart phrase is not commonly used. It can be employed to describe a state of being scared or afraid. For instance, someone makes a threat which another takes seriously such as that unless their job performance improves they will be fired from their job. The person so threatened would feel *sǐau jai*.

Timid Heart

jai sÒ   ใจเสาะ

For another example of a heart phrase used to describe behavior of someone experiencing a fearful situation, see the earlier definition of "timid heart."

Trembling Heart

ngan ngók tòk jai   งันงกตกใจ

An experience may be so intense and overwhelming that the person suffering actually trembles with fear. In the case of child abuse, where a child or relative inflicts mental or physical torture, the child would feel *ngan ngók tòk jai* as the person inflicting the punishment approached. In the case of a battered or abused wife, the abusive, violent husband who approaches the wife with his fist raised will cause her to feel *ngan ngók tòk jai*. Police officers or prison officials who use physical force to extract information from a suspect or prisoner, would find their charge trembling with fear as the beatings resumed.

Forgiveness
Return Heart

klàp jai   กลับใจ

When one person in a relationship feels they have hurt the other or mistaken their feelings toward another and seeks to repent of their error then he or she is *klàp jai.*

Hypocrisy
Mouth Not Straight with Heart

pàak kàp jai mây trong kan   ปากกับใจไม่ตรงกัน

Hypocrite Heart

pàak yàang jai yàang   ปากอย่างใจอย่าง

This is saying one thing and doing another. A powerful heart phrase to describe the hypocrite. A woman who tells her lover that he is the only person in the world for her, and the next day he sees her walking down the street with her arm wrapped around another man. Such a person will feel that this woman is *pàak kàp jai mây trong kan.* The heart phrase also comes in handy when dealing with the service providers. The computer shop that promises to have your computer system repaired on Thursday, and later explains next month has Thursdays as well. The travel agent who promises a ticket for one price and later requests an additional payment.

When Lek tells Noi that her dress is beautiful when in Lek's heart she feels the dress is so ugly it could be worn by a witch to a Halloween party, Lek is *pàak yàang jai yàang.* When an employer praises an employee for inferior work, that the employee knows is inferior, then later complains in an executive meeting that this employee is not doing good work, others may say that the employer is *pàak kàp jai mây trong kan.*

In a culture where saying "no" is difficult for many people, and saying "yes" is thought to please others and avoid confrontation, these heart phrases can be used to register the hypocrisy of a "yes" which is not really a "yes" but a "no".

Also the "hypocrite heart" phrases can be used to test another's sincerity and true intentions, by playfully asking whether the person is *pàak kàp jai mây trong kan* or *pàak yàang jai yàang.* Any time, in other words, the mouth is out of alignment with the heart—the possibilities are legion—this is a good heart phrase to remember.

Sweet Words But Want to Cut The Throat Heart

pàak praa sǎy jai chûeat khOO   ปากปราศรัยใจเชือดคอ

This Thai proverb is another heart phrase for hypocrisy. One maintains a calm, sweet exterior mask and speaks soothing words when inside the heart the speaker wishes to slit the throat of the other person. The employee who is disciplined in front of his or her colleagues and meekly admits the mistake but inside her or his heart is the desire to run a knife acorss the throat of her or his employer. Another example is Suporn's aunt is dying and Suporn is the principal beneficiary under her aunt's will. The aunt is a selfish, arrogant, bitter woman. When Suporn visits the aunt in the hospital she speaks sweetly to the dying woman while at the same time wishing the aunt would die.

Joy and Tenderness

Feelings of joy and tenderness in Thai are woven into a number of heart phrases. This section contains the verbal valentines that lovers, friends, and parents use all year round to express their positive, joyful, happy feelings, to convey a sense of well-being that another person is part of their life.

Appreciate Heart

sâap súeng jai   ซาบซึ้งใจ

súeng jai   ซึ้งใจ

When another person has assisted you in completing a job or with a project, then you feel *sâap súeng jai* toward that person. The heart phrase covers a broad range of conduct in which you are on the receiving end of helpfulness and for which you are grateful. Maybe you are lost in Bangkok and someone helps you find the place you are looking for on a map. Or you are at a phone booth and don't have the right change, and someone gives you the proper coins. In Thai, in other words, you appreciate acts of kindness from your heart.

Joyful Heart

chûuen jai   ชื่นใจ

When a person feels joy in their heart he or she experiences *chûuen jai*. How that joy enters the heart speaks volumes about the person. A man gives his a woman friend a gold chain and she feels *chûuen jai*. If someone wins the lottery they will likely feel *chûuen jai*. Or if you receive a pay rise or promotion at work, or if you are a student and do well in an examination or get a scholarship, the chances are you will feel *chûuen jai.*

Measure Heart

wát jai   วัดใจ

Similar expressions include *daw jai* ("guess heart"), *àan jai* ("read heart"), *lOOng jai* ("test heart"). The gist of each of these heart phrases is a description of the process of sizing up the qualities—spiritual, emotional, moral—possessed by another. When you meet another person, you take measure of (or guess, read or test, depending on the metaphor of choice) that person's heart. Similarly, if you are planning to enter into a close personal or business relationship with a Thai speaker, then he or she may ask themself about the nature of your heart. Is your heart true, small, mean, straight—these are a few of the possible metaphors applied to measure another's heart. The phrase represents an inner voice which tests the motives and goodwill of another person. In other words, are you a person they can trust? With this expression, you become a "Tailor of the Heart"—measuring every dimension and asking whether it fits the emotional requirements you feel are important.

Proper Heart

sŏm dang jai   สมดังใจ

The receiving of the thing you wished for is the essence of this heart phrase. For example, you receive a gift of flowers or a ticket to a concert from another person. You are the beneficiary of his or her act of kindness. Through such an act you obtain the thing you wished for. *sŏm dang jai* is a good feeling of possessing what you desire.

Remind Heart

tuean jai   เตือนใจ

There is an element of nostalgia in this heart phrase. A person misses their parents, or an old school friend. Another person may miss their wife or sweetheart, and when thoughts of the missed one—whom ever that might be—filter through a person's consciousness, he or she will feel *tuean jai.* Whether the absent person is at work or abroad, and your thoughts drift back to the good times and with anticipation of even better times to come.

Soft Heart

jai ÒOn ใจอ่อน

A person who has a soft heart for another—whether that person is a spouse, lover, children or parents or other category—then that person is *jai ÒOn*. The basic qualification is that the "soft hearted" person places another's welfare and happiness at a premium. Such a person communicates his or her feeling of another's importance through his or her words and deeds. The person on the receiving end of this communication feels they have priority in the life of the "soft hearted" person.

Straight Heart

trong hǔa jai ตรงหัวใจ

A person with a "straight heart" is direct in what they say. They make a point of saying it like it is, calling a spade a spade. This person shoots straight emotionally, but to shoot straight doesn't always mean flattery. It is the process and integrity which is at issue. When you tell your lover that you love her, you mean precisely that. This makes her feel happy. When you tell your lover you no longer love her, that's *trong hǔa jai*, too. Only the result is she may be unhappy. She feels happy or sad in heart. The phrase *trong hǔa jai* means the place where she feels her happiness or sadness.

Touch One to the Quick

jîi hǔa jai จี้หัวใจ

In this emotional state you may have "goose bumps" from a moving experience. It is likely that another person has done something to stir such feelings in you. You witness a special act of kindness, tenderness, goodness, or valor; something unexpected which has touched you emotionally. Perhaps you were at the cinema and a scene in a film made you feel sad or happy. If so, then you felt *jîi hǔa jai*. Perhaps you received flowers on your birthday from someone special. The feeling can be either an uplifting feeling or sad feeling. Either way you may feel *jîi hǔa jai*. The tone here requires some practice; *cîi* is pronounced like the Gee in the Bee Gees, the group which plays the kind of music which might make you feel *jîi hǔa jai*.

Pain and Sorrow

A person suffering wounds from the slings and arrows of a relationship will likely resort to one of these heart phrases.

The Thai language has evolved many heart phrases to express feelings of hurt, pain and sorrow. This is the heart vocabulary for injuries and harms that arise in personal relationships. One person has emotionally battered, let down, disappointed others. Like broken dreams, broken hearts are part of the human condition. These heart phrases may be accompanied by tears. Or, in some cases, physical violence. Here the feelings are often raw, open, and difficult for a person to bear.

Abrasive Heart

khàt jai　　ขัดใจ

The partner with an "abrasive heart" in the relationship is the one who constantly dictates to the other. This need to control and exercise authority makes such a person *khàt jai*. The person on the receiving end of the "abrasive hearted" person's stream of demands often feels an absence of personal freedom. Living with an "abrasive hearted" person is a little like living in a minimum security prison. The avenues of doing what one likes or wishes are closed. Using this heart phrase in describing another is the classic emotional reaction when a pushy person has pushed too hard, or too often or too far. The breaking point comes after such a person continues (after appropriate warnings) with a repeated string of requests, demands, and orders about all the small decisions in the relationship.

At Heart

trong hŭa jai　　ตรงหัวใจ

This heart phrase is an expression of feelings that can be either joyful or sorrowful depending on the person's reaction to another. We have previously dealt with the joyful side. Here is the dark, paintful side. The bad news that issues from *trong hŭa jai* will likely cause the listener suffering, anger, and pain. This is straight talking heart sending a message that may not be flattering even though it is truthful. Someone tells another they emotionally cold, unfeeling, or uncaring. These interpretations are not kept inside. The person with the "at heart" or "straight heart" lets his or her assessment be known.

Broken Heart

pen khây jai   เป็นไข้ใจ

Someone is in the process of breaking up with their lover and they both realize that the relationship has come to an end. The realization that it is over may cause them to feel *pen khây jai*. Their heart feels broken because the love they had cherished has vanished. Of course, the breaking of the heart is not limited to affairs of the heart. A person may have had their heart set on a particular career or job and what was sought after failed to materialize. Feeling the loss of such a dream is another reason to experience a "broken heart".

Bruised Heart

chám jai   ช้ำใจ

Someone says or does something that causes one to experience emotional pain. This feeling is *chám jai*. The degree of pain is directly related to the seriousness of the wrong felt. Sometimes it might be a minor slight—the husband forgets his wife's birthday, she feels *chám jai*. If the husband left his wife for another wife she might also feel *chám jai*—but the magnitude of pain is likely to be far greater.

Disheartened Heart

rá hěa jai   ระเหี่ยใจ

In a chronically bad relationship, you are always in conflict and argument with the other, and this makes you *rá hěa jai*. *phǔa mia ra hěa jai* is a Thai saying for a husband and wife who are at one another's throats. It is the ultimate condemnation in a culture that places high value on social unity, consensus and order.

Hurt Heart

jèp chám nám jai   เจ็บช้ำน้ำใจ

This is another of the "big hurt" category of heart phrases. A major emotional blow has been dealt in order to resort to this version of "hurt heart." For instance, Lek is a university student and is informed by her teacher that she has failed her final year and will not graduate with her class. She aks her friend Charles to help her with English. He fails to assist her and again, Lek feels *jèp chám nám jai*. To make matters even worse, having failed university, Lek's job offer is terminated, her father cuts off her allowance, and again she feels "hurt heart" by this string of reversals. Finally, her best friend who does graduate, no longer has time for Lek, fails to phone her or invite her out as in the past. Lek, in each example, feels *jèp chám nám jai.*

Master of Heart

pen jâw hǔa jai   เป็นเจ้าหัวใจ

"Master heart" is a common Thai heart phrase. It arises in the context of power struggles within the home, family, and office. A person who is subject to the control of someone else where that person uses the control and authority to limit one's freedom may well hear this heart phrase use. It is not a compliment. This is a bad news heart message. If someone complains about feeling *pen jâw hǔa jai,* it means another person has been pushing wants, demands, desires onto them. Sending out messages such as: change your hair style, change your clothes, shoes or the way you walk and talk. The "master of heart" is a dictator and lacks a respect for the freedom of others. If you are on the wrong side of a control freak, this is the heart phrase you are screaming to get out of his or her sight.

Moody Heart

ngùt ngìt jai   หงุดหงิดใจ

Anyone can feel moody when something has not gone the way one had wished. A person with a "moody heart" is in a different category. Such a person with a generally moody nature is described as *khîi ngùt ngìt.* Such a person is easily upset with small, minor things. People, kids, dogs all get on their nerves. These things are too big, too small, too dirty, demanding; and they can't accommodate all the demands life makes on them. They normally react with a foul mood and anger. If this is your personality type, or one possessed by someone you know, then the chances are you will hear another refer to you or to one of your actions as *ngùt ngìt jai.*

Pain Heart

jèp jai   เจ็บใจ

When a person has rejected someone, a lover, a friend, or employee, the other person, the one who is rejected, is liable to feel *jèp jai.* This heart phrase can be the siren and flashing red light of an emotional emergency vehicle. "Pain hearted" people feel flares-up of real pain, and they are often under considerable emotional distress. To hear this heart phrase is a signal that something is about to break inside the person; and that something may be their ability to control their emotions. "Pain heart" may be translated into action; it can become the prelude to a serious emotional scene, and in some cases, physical confrontation. When someone tells you made them *jèp jai*, it is time to exit, or invest in a bulletproof vest.

Pierced Heart

chÔOk chám rá kam jai   ชอกช้ำระกำใจ

This is another variation of broken heart. Though here the degree of sadness is of a higher intensity. On a misery scale of one to ten, this heart phrase ranks about a 8.9. The heart phrase is used for the major moments of sadness and misery in one's life. For instance, the wife of a taxi driver who claims to have found and returned to the rightful owner a large sum of cash which the owner accidentally left at the airport. As a result of his actions, the driver is treated as a hero. Only the driver's story turns out to be false. The driver's wife upon learning of his deception and arrest would feel *chÔOk chám rákam jai*.

Sad Heart

sâw jai   เศร้าใจ

The machinery of joy and hope breaks down. Some experience is causing one to suffer from a broken heart condition. "Sad heart" is similar in meaning to *hŭa jai ráthom*. The "sad hearted" person is miserable, feeling emotional pain. In this emotional state, the "sad heart" doesn't want to get out of bed, wishing the world and all its problems as well as their own would fly away like a bad dream. A person can have *sâw jai* over the news that another person has suffered a major accident or loss, or over news of a crime or misdeed that has caused innocent people to suffer. A "sad heart" occurs when hearing news that a building has collapsed killing a hundred people, or a hotel catches on fire, killing many people, or, for the business person with US dollar loans, when he or she learns that the Thai baht has dropped more than 25% in value.

Steal Heart

thûuk khamooy jai pay   ถูกขโมยใจไป

One person does not know or is unaware that another person loves him or her. In this situation, the ignored person, the one who is in love, feels painfully alone. "Steal heart" is the Thai version of unrequited love. The person who experiences this one-sided love may confide his or her condition to a friend. Seeking advice about unrequited love is a way of dealing with this kind of heart condition. What is certain is that such a person is unhappy because he or she feels *thûuk khamooy jai pay* and seeking relief in friendship is a common way of dealing with the problem.

Turn Your Stomach Heart

jèp thÓOng khÔOng jai   เจ็บท้องข้องใจ

Something has happened tht causes one to feel pain. The pain can be either physical or mental. A person who is beaten by a mugger for his or her wallet, will feel *jèp thÓOng khÔOng jai*. Thus "stomach ache" is a metaphor for every kind of injury. It does not necessarily mean the pain is literally in the stomach. The driver in a traffic accident who receives an injury to his arm is *jèp thÓOng khÔOng jai*. A police officer giving a traffic ticket to an offender makes the offender feel *jèp thÓOng khÔOng jai*.

Very Tired Heart

nùeay jai thÊEp khàat   เหนื่อยใจแทบขาด

You have the kind of bad relationship suggested by *phǔa mia rahǎa jai*. You and your spouse have been at one another's throats for a substantial period of time. The wearing down of each other emotionally will make both of you *nùeay jai thÊEp khàat* about the relationship. The phrase concerns emotional exhaustion. It is a kind of burn-out feeling which comes from keeping strong emotions at a high boil for a long period of time. Another meaning is broader and applies to anyone who feels tired after a long day at work.

Wretched Heart

trOOm jai   ตรอมใจ

To experience *trOOm jai* is to enter into a state of profound unhappiness and despair. For instance, a couple have been married for two years and are very much in love. One day on the way to the office, the husband is killed in a road accident. The widow, in these circumstances, would experience *trOOm jai*. The grief is so large that she feels that she will die. The essence of "wretched heart" is the scale of the misery. The heart phrase is confined to extreme circumstances, where the person is totally overwhelmed by a profound sense of sadness.

There are a number of heart expressions which convey the desire to allow another person have their way. Whether this is viewed as pleasing or spoiling the person depends on the nature of the relationship between the person granting permission and the person receiving it as well as the context in which it occurs. The heart phrases arise also in circumstances where there is a conflict of desire and one person yields to the wishes of the other.

Follow Heart

taam jai   ตามใจ

You want to permit someone to have their own way, allow them to make a choice or decision, e.g., the movie, the restaurant, the holiday destination. By giving the other person the freedom to choose, you are in effect saying to the other person *taam chÔOp jai* or follow your heart. At the same time, you are giving up your own choice over the matter and following along with the wishes of another. While the literal translation is follow as you like your own heart, or you go ahead and do what you think is the right thing to do. Also, it can mean that you are spoiling or indulging another person.

Granting Wish Heart

yàang jai   อย่างใจ

You wish to make another's wish or desire come true and you grant them permission or actively help them achieve their desire. Perhaps you have a wish you want for yourself. Building a new house. Completing university. Traveling to Canada. You may want to grant the wish inside your own heart or for another. The meaning comes close to spoiling another person by granting them their desire.

Please Heart

aw jai   เอาใจ

This is the kind of person who makes a special effort to bring home a small gift for your wife and child. It might be a special sweet or flowers or the latest video. In doing so they give a constant reminder of their affection for them. Small gestures such as allowing another to watch a TV program when you would rather watch the news. In a restaurant, ordering the sea bass on the menu because you know that this is your friend's favourite dish. You *aw jai* your spouse or child with the gift. The same principle applies if you give presents to your lover. You *aw jai* that person or please him or her with the gift. *aw jai* is a common heart expression. And the idea of gift giving as a form of *aw jai* is a part of the Thai tradition.

Respecting Others
Mind and Spirit Heart

jìt jai   จิตใจ

Life, Mind and Spirit Heart

chii wít jìt jai   ชีวิตจิตใจ

The essence of *cìt jai* as a general heart phrase is a mental state where one is thinking or feeling. It is what is going on inside one's head or heart from moment to moment. One is always in one state of *jìt jai* or another in the sense that we are what our mind is. *chii wít jìt jai* focuses more on living or existence. In usage, *chii wít jìt jai* covers the notion that other people have value and are entitled to be treated with due regard. *chii wít jìt jai* is violated when one's employer treats them as a machine rather than as a human being. As in the case of a factory where the employees are held as virtual slaves. The employee suffering from mistreatment will feel that they have been robbed of their *jìt jai*. These heart phrases are broad enough to encompass the treatment of animals, where the person abusing or beating an animal is said to ignore the animal's *jìt jai*. All creatures in the *jìt jai* universe are entitled to respect and life and fair treatment.

Revealing The Heart

Before examing the many heart phrases that address secrets of the heart, there is one phrase that used as the pathway to uncover these secrets.

Revealing Heart

jÒ jai   เจาะใจ

The metaphor is to "drill" into another's heart in order to unearth the rich ore of secrets locked inside. The name of a popular Thai TV show is *jÒ jai*. The participants on this TV show are asked to reveal something about themselves that they haven't exposed to anyone else. *jÒ jai* is used as verb in the context of extracting the revealing information. An informal cross-examination of another's secret past. For instance, Noi places advertisements on the internet seeking to meet a husband. She receives many emails in response. She forms a correspondence with several pen pals around the world. Three of them begin to send her money on a monthly basis, thus improving Noi's standard of living. Noi's best friend notices the extra money and asks Noi to reveal the source. Noi then reveals her internet pen pal scheme. In this instance, Noi's friend has *jÒ jai* Noi.

Hidden Deep in the Heart
lúek lúek nay jai   ลึกลึกในใจ

The secret inside may well be from a past relationship. The woman who has left her lover of many years and though she finds a new lover, the secret of her prior love burns deep inside her heart. This is a secret that she cannot reveal or express to her new lover. This is particularly poignant if the reason for the departure was death or for reasons other than hostility. The secret of that lost love remains locked in the heart forever no matter what loves comes afterwards. "Hidden deep inside the heart" is similar to the western notion of first love. In this case, though, it is first love of such a deep and profound nature that revealing it would cause problems in the new relationship.

Keeping Thoughts within the Heart
âEp mii jai   แอบมีใจ

The best example of this phrase is the unexpressed feelings that one may have for another person. At the office, one person may have a romantic interest in her or his co-worker. But the person having these feelings will not let the other know how she or he truly feels. Indeed, he or she may go out of their way to mask those feelings.

Secret Heart
am phraang jai   อำพรางใจ

In Thailand, listening to Thai music, one hears *am phraang jai* in Thai torch songs. This feeling is the opposite of *pòet jai* พูดใจ or open heart. The person with a "secret heart" has likely invented a fantasy relationship with another. There is no disclosure to others, the secret is kept locked in. Such a person may be in love with the beautiful secretary in the office but he is too shy to ask her name. But inside his heart he may have invented an entire relationship with her. Not that he would ever disclose this secret life. He keeps his feelings locked deep inside his heart.

Secret Pain in the Heart

hǔa jai kèp kòt หัวใจเก็บกด

One may experience any number of negative emotions such as anger, frustration, depression, disappointment but rather than expressing them openly these feelings are buried deeply inside the person who feels them. This heart phrase is akin to the English notion of the stiff upper lip. Not complaining about setbacks in life but getting on with it. Lek has studied very hard during her term at university. She is serious and doesn't go out on the party circuit with her less serious friends even though she is frequently invited to join them. Lek is sad because she cannot participate in the fun times with her friends. She wants to talk about her feelings openly to her friends, about her conflict with her desire to study for an examination, but she keeps this conflict inside herself, smiles at her friends and says she cannot go because she has a headache.

Trust and Importance

There are many *heart* expressions used by Thai speakers to express their feelings of trust and commitment to their partner in a relationship. These heart phrases include faithfulness and openness in the relationship. Some of the heart phrases are often used in a parent/child relationship. Others are used in many different personal contexts, touching upon special feelings of intimacy, fate, honesty and certainty of commitment.

Believe Heart

chûea jai เชื่อใจ

plong jai chûea ปลงใจเชื่อ

A person using "believe heart" is requesting another to have faith that his or her intentions, explanations, or decisions are made in good faith and are honest and reliable. There may be money missing from the petty cash box, and the boss suspects an employee of taking it. The employee may respond with a plea of innocence, asking the boss to believe that he is telling the truth. He asks the boss to believe that he is speaking honorably from the heart. The boyfriend has come back at three in the morning, and asks his girlfriend to believe that he was attending a seminar on company law. He is asking her to "believe heart" or *chûea jai*.

Beloved Heart

sǎay jai   สายใจ

The state of being *sǎay jai* is mostly felt in the relationship between a mother and child. Another more literal translation would be "Chain of the Heart." The heart phrase reflects a combination of duty, love and obligation toward a child, and demonstrates that the mother truly cares about his or her wellbeing. Such a mother feels that her sons and daughters are a permanent and essential feature of her emotional life. She includes these people in her thoughts and actions; their feelings matter to her. She also may have *sǎay jai* feelings about a friend, lover, or parents.

Body and Heart

tháng kaay lÉ jai   ทั้งกายและใจ

"Body and heart" feels as if they are one or merged in the loving relationship. The separation with another has evaporated in a shared feeling of oneness. A melodic tenor sax is playing in the background. You are in a beach cottage at Koh Samui with that special person. It is sunset and together, on the beach, you watch the sun going down over the sea. At that moment, you have a sense of loving each other body and soul. This is one step beyond *plong jai rák* You have given your whole body and soul to another.

Close to Heart

sanìt jai   สนิทใจ

A person who feels they can expose their deepest nature and share their private interior life with another will experience the feelings associated with "close to heart". When you feel close to a friend or lover, the sense of closeness is *sanìt jai*. The feelings are warm, intimate, gentle arising from a true sense of closeness. This heart phrase (commonly used) is often used to describe feelings of close personal intimacy with another. The scope for such feelings of intimacy are not limited to husband and wife or boyfriend and girlfriend and include a large range of relationships such as friends, parents, colleagues, fellow Thai speakers, or religious leaders.

Confident Heart

mân jai มั่นใจ

This is a confident feeling a person may have about themselves, or others, or to deal with the situation they face. A person may feel confident about his or her abilities as a driver, in a tennis game, in learning a language or in mastering social skills. Or such a person may feel that another person can be trusted completely. You are a long way down the road in any relationship when you feel it is *mân jai*. You only will feel that you are *mân jai* at the point that all misgivings, doubt, and mistrust have disappeared. At this point your heart is confident about the other person and you have achieved intimacy.

Fate Heart

duang jai ดวงใจ

The notion of destiny and fate is strong in the Thai culture. There are many expressions which incorporate the word *duang*. A child is *duang jai* of his mother. This means the child is the most important and loved person for the mother; she feels in her heart these things about her child. Also the phrase can be applied to relationships between father and child; boyfriend and girlfriend; and husband and wife. In the case of romantic relationships, there is the poetic idea of fate or destiny bringing the couple together. Perhaps they had a relationship in a prior life.

Gold Chain Around One's Heart

sôo thOOng khlÓOng jai โซ่ทองคล้องใจ

This heart phrase expresses the feeling parents often have about their children who are in an orbit around their lives. You hold your baby in your arms and you know this feeling of the baby being a circle around your heart. The feeling is a special, usually family, emotion which recognizes the closeness of hearts in shared lives. It is a good feeling, a feeling better than gold.

Iris of the Heart

kÊEw taa duang jai แก้วตาดวงใจ

The metaphor is from the eye of the beholder. The heart phrase translates as the most important thing inside one's heart. It is common for Thais to say the most important people in a mother's heart are her children. And conversely, a daughter and most sons will invariably say their mother is the most important thing in their heart. It is an essential feature of Thai culture that the mother occupies the center of what is good, pure, kind, untainted; and motherhood is highly valued and admired by Thai women.

Irrevocable Heart

plong jai rák   ปลงใจรัก

When a person has made that a final, ultimate commitment to another—in the sense that there is no pulling back, no second thoughts or changing your mind—then this irreversible feeling of love is *plong jai rák*. The heart phrase might be used in situations other than a personal relationship and include feelings towards another person's country or an association of friends. The words are powerful in the degree of intensity because they convey a forever quality of the feeling. Thus an "irrevocable heart" is one that is committed for the long term.

One Heart

jai deaw   ใจเดียว

The man or woman who is and remains faithful to their partner has *jai deaw*. In the "one heart" there is only one room. Enough space for one special person to occupy. This heart phrase is closely linked with the concept of monogamy. At the opposite scale is the "butterfly" who flies from lover to lover as if they were flowers in a field. The butterfly does not have "one heart". Another example of usage would be if Ning's husband dies and she does not seek another husband or partner she also may be said to possess *jai deaw*. Having "one heart" is a phrase commonly heard in conversations about relationships.

Open Heart

pòet jai   เปิดใจ

When two people are close enough as to disclose their most secret, hidden feelings to each other, then they are *pòet jai*. It may also apply outside an intimate relationship, to an entertainer, such as a singer, who has created a bond with his or her audience. *pòet jai* is probably the best translation for the English phrase: *heart-to-heart talk*.

Person with Trust Heart

phûu thîi wáy jai   ผู้ที่ไว้ใจ

When you trust someone completely you can speak from your heart to her or him; then you have *phûu thîi wáy jai*. For most Thais, the mother is someone they can speak their true heart to. You can have *phûu thîi wáy jai* with a mother, a child, or a very good friend. This is your true confident, the person who you think will always be there for you, never turn away from you in life. It may be difficult for some to include their lovers or spouses in this category.

Same Heart

jai deaw kan   ใจเดียวกัน

jai deaw kan is something you should have with your spouse or lover. The heart phrase may generate positive, good feelings of enjoying a shared view of life with another. There is an absence of conflict over choices to be made. You like the same movies, food, friends, holidays. You both drink *fresh squeezed orange juice and put strawberry jam on your wholewheat toast while* listening to old *Rolling Stones* songs. You both have the same favorite color, and prefer a hard mattress to a soft one. At the same time, there is a negative side to this heart phrase. It is possible to experience *jai deaw kan* with a total stranger. For example, you may wish to have an aisle seat on a flight from Bangkok to New York City but a stranger wants it too. Through a mistake, the seat is double-booked. Your desire of wanting the same seat creates a state of competition, and this common desire or hunger for the same object cause one's heart to feel the hard edge of "same heart".

Straight Heart

jai trong kan   ใจตรงกัน

This has the same meaning as *jai deaw kan* and can be used in the same context, e.g., to indicate emotional closeness and bonding with another person, or the competition with a stranger who shares your preference for an object of your desire. The essence of "straight heart" is the direct, honest expression of feelings. Nothing is hidden or locked away.

Sure Heart

nÊE jai แน่ใจ

This is another heart phrase for those with self-assurance about themselves and actions. In a relationship, when you are certain about your feelings toward another, you can say you feel *nÊE jai*. In other contexts, you may use the expression to signal your self-assured decision or opinion, whether it is to purchase a new shirt, to order a new item from the menu, or the entertainment value of a film. *mân jai*, like *nÊE jai*, refers to an emotional state of confidence of action and plans for action, as well as to a feeling about another person or object.

Tie Heart

mát jai มัดใจ

phùuk jai ผูกใจ

The heart phrase "Tie Heart" includes behavior tailored to make another feel the tug of obligations and the weight of duties which should be honored. The essence of this heart phrase is a course of behavior designed to bind another emotionally to a person. A Thai wife might try to *mát jai* the husband by cooking elaborate meals or in her selection of dress and makeup. A husband may give his wife diamonds and gold on a regular basis. Such activity creates bonds of obligation and affection, and may assist in maintaining the loyalty of the other person.

Trust Blindly Heart

taay jai ตายใจ

Your views, decisions, wishes, and explanations are accepted by another person in a relationship without questioning them. A person may decide to move the family to another house. The wife and children trust the father's decision. The mother decides to change her son's school, the son and father implicitly trust her decision. The office worker who arrives home at three in the morning and gives the explanation that he was in a business meeting may seek to draw upon the "trust blindly heart" of his wife. If his wife trusts him, then she is likely to feel *taay jai*. But if he comes home at three in the morning two nights in a row, *taay jai* will likely not be the response. She may also question whether he has "one heart".

Try Another's Heart
lOOng jai ลองใจ

The heart must make choices, and feelings and loyalties about our obligations to others (as well as to ourselves) inform the choices that are made. Whatever choice is made may cause another to try our hearts. This occurs because there is a conflict in what is the right thing to do, and the person testing your heart is seeking to determine his or her importance in the larger scheme of things. The person whose heart is tried, feels torn, undecided. This heart phrase is addressed at the person is doing the testing. When your wife says to you, "You can go out on the town with your friends, or stay home and help me wallpaper the living room." She is testing your feelings about her. She is *lOOng jai* in this testing of your heart.

What's in One's Heart
khwaam nay jai ความในใจ

This heart phrase means that you are speaking with honesty and truth from your heart. One uses the phrase in circumstances that are similar to *pòet jai*. A person is not using deceit or lies to mask their real feelings about something or someone. They have *khwaam nay jai* when there are no barriers blocking the truth from being expressed, and no fear from saying what one honestly feels to another.

Unity
Association from the Heart
khóp kan dûay jai คบกันด้วยใจ

Associations amongst people of different social rank or class is sometimes difficult. Where there are two people, one poor and the other rich, yet despite this difference they form and maintain a friendship. One can be friends with someone who comes from a different background, religion, or ethnic group. They can experience an "association of the heart" which allows them to overcome such differences. This is not a surface or pretend association but one that is sincere.

Confederate Heart

phûu rûam jai   ผู้ร่วมใจ

When a person has been in a relationship for sometime it is natural for him or her to develop a close, intimate bond with other person. Using an internet metaphor, such a person is special and the emotional frequency has a wider bandwidth. Less is held back. There is no problem logging on to the other person's emotional wave-length. More feelings are transmitted faster and more accurately. They are a confederate in life; a confederate of the heart. The heart phrase is an expression of a high degree of bonding with another person. You may have many friends and relationships but it is rare that you will have the feeling toward that other person of *phûu rûam jai*.

Harmony Heart

nám nùeng jai deaw kan   น้ำหนึ่งใจเดียวกัน

This heart phrase is used to describe people who can work together. "Harmony heart" is used among friends, colleagues or members of the same sports team. The common element is the ability of these people to feel unity and a shared sense of common purpose. Managers or senior executives of companies as well as coaches have the responsibility for creating this feeling of "harmony heart" and the extent they succeed, the better the performance of those working for them is likely to be.

United Heart

rûam jai   ร่วมใจ

This is the verb form of the close bond of working with another. See *phûu rûam jai*.

Vulnerability

Vulnerable Heart

jai bÒOp baang   ใจบอบบาง

Vulnerability of the heart means someone is easily hurt. Life with such a person is not always easy. To make such a person happy and content means that one must take care of his or her every wish and desire. If, for whatever reason, one should fail to do what he or she wants, then the results are predictable. The person with the vulnerable heart may sulk or cry. They have been offended by the failure of the other to keep them satisfied.

Heart Talk
in Society

Chapter 6

In the Thai language, the relationships formed in the larger context of family, friends, business, job, and school are reflected in heart phrases. There are a wide range of feelings found in these heart phrases. Some examples include emotional pushes and pulls, seductions, fears, pride, surprises and changes which come from an encounter or experience with another person. Some of the heart phrases will have appeared in earlier chapters in other situations. It is, however, important to remember the use of the same heart phrase with an employer carries a different emotional message than one delivered by a mother to a child.

This chapter exposes more of the public face of the heart. While in the West matters of the heart are often viewed as private matters, in the Thai language the basic social interaction with strangers, government officials, colleagues, friends, business associates is defined by the heart. It is beyond the scope of this small book to analyse fully how the private and public world of heart shapes the network of all relationships. The goal of looking how the heart phrases are used in society is more modest. It provides a start for exploration of how the language of heart starts to explain the nature of Thai society and culture.

Class System

A heart vocabulary is needed to understand the way people behave with others of different social rank within the Thai class system. In general, the Thai class structure has retained certain features associated with a feudalistic system. Patrons and benefactors have traditionally exchanged protection for loyalty and other benefits. This is less about friendship but power arrangements distributed in such a fashion that there is often little choice but to fit into the existing class system. Though the system is gradually changing as calls for political change suggest a restructuring of the old social arrangement may come soon.

Awe Heart

kreeng jai   เกรงใจ

There are few heart phrases more difficult to translate and explain. And there may be no other heart phrase more important than "awe heart" which is the heart of hearts of the Thai system. The phrase reflects something—a mingling of reverence, respect, deference, homage and fear—which every Thai person feels toward someone who is their senior, their boss, their teacher, mother and father, a police officer or those who are perceived to be a member of a higher social class. In practice, a person with "awe heart" would be inhibited from questioning or criticizing. "Awe heart" is about acceptance of what those in authority say, do, and decide. And hoping for the best.

One of the first songs schoolchildren learn is about the importance of *kreeng jai*. To say that someone knows *kreeng jai* is to confer a substantial compliment. That is, to be submissive to authority. To smile and never complain and to never reveal feelings of disappointment or frustration. The public mask must, in other words, be one of perfect contentment. On the opposite side, to say that someone does not know or practice *kreeng jai* is a major insult. This person soon is labelled a trouble maker and is marginalized.

"Awe heart" remains a core *jai* expression that also accounts for what appears on the surface as an incredible degree of politeness and civility found in exchanges between Thai people. A sense of face is also involved in this phrase. The social rank and class rank is mapped, or better, encoded in "awe heart". It defines the way that people between various ranks communicate, behave, and react with one another. It defines also their expectations about the range of behavior to be received from others.

"Awe heart" marks the social boundaries in a highly class-structured system where the sense of station and relationship to others is keenly felt and respected. *kreeng jai* also means a display of considerations between those of unequal social rank, whether in the home or workplace. An employer would demonstrate considerate behavior toward an employee or servant, and the employee or servant reciprocates with a display of considerate behavior toward the employer.

This definition merely touches the surface of "awe heart" which is part creation of social theatre with the accompanying masks to be worn, the script to be read, and the part to be played. The drama of "awe heart" is played out throughout Thailand twenty-four hours a day. Whenever two Thai speakers meet, the drama begins.

Good Heart

jai dii   ใจดี

A person who is *jai dii* has a kind and generous nature. For example, when a mother takes her children shopping or to see a movie, the children think she is *jai dii*. The heart phrase expresses a state of being of goodness, or doing something for another without being asked. The emphasis is on the action which has not been asked for. "Good heart" can be understood as a key component of *the kreeng jai* world of reciprocal social obligations. *kreeng jai* makes it awkward (even painful) to ask or request something from someone of higher rank. The smiling mask of contentment would have to be dropped. Many are not prepared to make themselves so vulnerable.

There are, however, indirect ways of communicating such desires. When the thing wished for comes without a request, then the person conferring it is *jai dii*. To have asked for something directly risks a loss of face: the person asked may say "no". Thus desires or wishes are often left unexpressed—at least directly—and a high value is placed on a person who has the ability to read such desires and wishes and grant them without a request.

Justice Heart

mii jai pen tham   มีใจเป็นธรรม

It is in the nature of some people to seek justice for others. A person with a "justice heart" feels upset and concerned when they see other people who are suffering, living in poverty, or helpless in the face of adversity. They sense the unfairness about the way resources and benefits and opportunities are distributed. The lack of justice in such a distribution disturbs their *mii jai pen tham* nature. The person with a "justice heart" has a social conscience and does not wear blinkers when confronted with the unfairness and injustice that goes on around them.

Push Heart

khěn jai   เข็ญใจ

In the times of plenty, those feeling the "push heart" are off in the margin. When the economy as a whole plunges and many people have lost money, land, cars and jobs, the number of people who feel stranded in an improvised life without the resources to lift oneself out and into a better life increases dramatically. The emotional tone is one associated with a bad feeling. The destitute person feels they will never have enough money for a better life.

Seduce Heart

lÔO jai ล่อใจ

Used as a verb, "seduce heart" applies to one who is making an emotional bribe. This heart phrase can have the softer meaning of "promoting" the feeling in another to want or desire an object or person. The object or person desired operates to tempt (perhaps through an effective advertisement) a person. Once tempted, the person desires to possess the person or object; this burning desire for the object or other person makes the person with the craving or desire look at the person firing up his appetite as making a seduction. The seduction is not necessarily sexual. For example, it can also be a kind of incentive to make others work harder; the bonus for productive work acts as *lÔO jai* for the employees, who desire the extra cash.

Seduction Machine Heart

khrûeang lÔO jai เครื่องล่อใจ

This is the noun form of *lÔO jai*. What machinery seduces an individual heart is wide and varied. The seduction of owning and being seen in the presence of a BMW, Rolex watch, gold and diamonds, an estate in France, an apartment in London is *khrûeang lÔO jai* for many people. These objects are the "seduction machine of the heart" driving the person who wants to possess such things with a lusty desire to acquire and retain them.

Stamp Heart

prà tháp jai ประทับใจ

You feel impressed or *pratháp jai* with the person who has the nature of *jìt jai sǔung*. The person might be a religious leader, scholar, or a community leader. If he or she appears to you as *hǔa sǔung*—a polished, well-dressed and elegant person—you might be impressed by the display but not necessarily by the real nature of the person lurking behind the display. This phrase is a basis for judging how people judge the character of others. There is a broader meaning to the phrase. You say you feel *pratháp jai* or impressed with the food, climate, kindness, and smiles you find in Thailand.

Tall Heart

jìt jai sǔung   จิตใจสูง

jìt jai sǔung refers to the nature of a person who has high moral standards. "Tall heart" is the difference between moral richness and material richness, and Thai speakers are able to distinguish between the two cases. *hǔa sǔung* refers to a person who is well-dressed, who puts on the appearance of being well off by possessing expensive clothes, expensive car, mobile phone, Rolex watch and other symbols associated with the rich. This is a description of a person who is attached to such objects of wealth, and displays the wealth but underneath the display there is no evidence of the high moral standards attached to *jìt jai sǔung*. This is another part of the social "awe heart" social drama. The costumes of the actors along with their masks can distract attention away from the true nature of the person behind the costume and mask.

Thank You Heart

khÒOp jai   ขอบใจ

This heart phrase which simply means "thank you" should be used with caution by a foreigner because it might create the impression that the foreigner considers himself or herself in a higher social class. It implies a superior/inferior social relationship or, between people of equal social rank, is a sign of age difference. For example, it might be used by someone senior to express his or her appreciation to someone who is their junior. It is another example of the way the social system is ordered in Thailand. It is best avoided by foreigners and is a lesson of where the simple words "thank you" convey a powerful social message. It is better to express thank you with *khòop khun*.

Wake-up Heart

plùk jai   ปลุกใจ

A person who has radical views about the fairness of the government, social class, and the political system possesses a "wake-up heart". Such a person announces their own version of Utopia for the masses, and expects them to wake up to their call for radical change in the structure of the way things are. *plùk jai* is the wake-up call issued by a revolutionary. Of course what one group or individual views as radical might be viewed by others as a fair, just realignment of the political and economic structure and not radical at all.

Wholeheartedness

samàk jai   สมัครใจ

The idea behind "wholeheartedness" is the act of volunteering to something. The good deed has not been demanded or required by the person on the receiving end. Small acts of kindness fall within this heart phrase. Thus an employee who places fresh cut flowers on his or her boss's desk exhibits a "wholeheartedness". Such a person, in Thai culture, has displayed *samàk jai*. The emphasis is on a willingness to do more than is required, to volunteer time and energy, resulting in making the lives of those around them more pleasant and comfortable.

Community

Appropriate Heart

jai dii kÊE dâay jai ráay kÊE mǎy   ใจดีแก้ได้ ใจร้ายแก้ไหม

The literal translation is "good heart unties thread, cruel heart unties silk." The heart phrase is another example of a Thai proverb used to describe group or community activity. The rural texture of the phrase should not be thought of as a limitation for a more general usage. In essence, this phrase means that work is best given to people who have the capability of performing the task or assignment, and withheld from those who cannot efficiently do the work. Thus the person who is able to unite the thread may be unable to untie the silk. Conversely, the person who is good at untying silk may be inept at untying thread. Within the context of a company, factory, school or sports team, those who make the assignments should attempt to take into account the individual strengths and weaknesses of those under their charge. The heart phrase also applies at the political level. A person without any experience or training in economics would make a poor appointment as Finance Minister or the head of the Bank of Thailand. A person appointed to be Minister of Justice who has no legal training would likely be ineffectively in carrying out the responsibilities of his or her job.

Heart Joining Heart

jai prà săan jai ใจประสานใจ

This is the title of a well-known Thai song. *jai prà säan jai* is sung whenever there is a special occasion with lots of Thais in attendance. For instance, it is traditional to sing it on New Year's Eve, at the end of a regional sporting event among the Thai participants, and at special occasions at school. The song creates a strong sense of community spirit. The lyric evokes a number of strong emotions such as feelings of friendship, understanding, love, harmony, and unity. The message conveyed by the lyric is that people share and belong to a large community of people who are held together by these feelings. It is an inspirational song that many Thais know by heart but few foreigners are aware of *jai prà säan jai*.

Important Issue Heart

khÔO yày jai khwaam ข้อใหญ่ใจความ

This heart phrase usually appears in writing. Certain public or community issues or problems provide the subject matter or context for usage. For instance, funding for education, road construction, oil tax increases, gun control, environmental issues such as pollution are issues that are *khÔO yày jai khwaam* for a large number of people.

Consensus
Agree Heart

yin yOOm phrÓOm jai ยินยอมพร้อมใจ

Consensus building is the essence of this heart phrase. The agreement or consensus to be reached may be among friends as to which restaurant or movie to go to for an evening of relaxation. *yin yOOm phrÓOm jai* occupies an important role within the family unit as well. The family as a unit reaches a decision to sell a plot of land or shares in a family owned company, or to send a son or daughter abroad for education. In a number of cases, the decision to marry falls within the general consensus of the family. There is a strong impetus to act in concert with the approval or consent of friends and family. Decision-making, in other words, is less individualistic and there are always attempts to take into account the feelings and desires of the group.

Cooperative Heart

rûam rEEng rûam jai   ร่วมแรงร่วมใจ

The emphasis is on cooperation among friends, colleagues and family to roll up their sleeves to accomplish a joint task or project. A group of friends may hire a bus and go to an upcountry temple to make merit. In the workplace, on a marketing plan a group of five co-workers, all assigned a part of the project, must work together in a cooperative spirit to ensure that the project is completed on schedule and in accordance with the objectives set by the boss. In certain cases, however, the "cooperative heart" may not be present. The chronic Bangkok traffic problem is, in part, caused by too many government agencies, departments, and committees involved in the process of solving the traffic problem, and it is difficult under those circumstances for the people involved to *rûam rEEng rûam jai.*

Differences

Distinctive Heart

tôn máy tàng plÔOng phîi   ต้นไม้ต่างปล้อง
nÓOng tàng jai   พี่น้องต่างใจ

This is from a Thai proverb to the effect that as each piece of wood is distinctive, each older and younger sibling is different, too. "Distinctive hearts" recognizes that it is natural for there to be a divulgence of taste, likes, dislikes, talents, personality, and temperament among members of the same family.

Friendship

Friendship is an important release from formal behavior demanded from the "awe heart" world of those who are older, more powerful, or occupy a higher social rank. Not surprisingly the heart phrases honor this freedom of being with one's friends and by understanding the range of these expressions, some of the emotional expectations of friendship are revealed.

Accomplice Heart

pen jai   เป็นใจ

Not all friendship is for the betterment of society or the community. Criminals have friends who are usually other criminals. The "accomplice heart" is the secret alliance between people who set out to accomplish a mission. It does not have to be a major crime like a bank robbery. For example, the person seated in the back of the car may look the other way as the chauffeur runs a red light or double parks. Or two crooks may be *pen jai* and decide to rob people on a *soi*. The spin is on a kind of conspiracy between two people to deceive, cheat, or allow another do something which is morally suspect or illegal. Thus the "accomplice heart" is not always about friendship. It may be passive behavior. One person simply looks the other way and by doing so indirectly encourages the immoral or illegal act.

Cheer-on Heart

aw jai chûay   เอาใจช่วย

Friendship is about supporting your friends, urging them on to success or victory. You *aw jai chûay* your friend to be a winner. It is expected that a friend will show his friendship by rooting for his or her friend, family, school, club or business to win in a contest. The heart phrase refers to the friend's position as a cheerleader on the sidelines of the contest and who gives encouragement, support, and applause. The "cheer-on-heart" provides a morale boost through active support and encouragement.

Considerate Heart

mii kâE jai   มีแก่ใจ

Friendship is about rendering assistance when a friend is having a problem or experiencing trouble. When a difficult situation arises, and the problem persists, one friend comes to the assistance of the person with a problem. She or he is *mii kâE jai* in helping the person in need. This action is the opposite of self-centered, selfish behavior. A person with a "considerate heart" takes another person's feelings of frustration, gloom and doom to heart, and stands ready, willing, and able to give support.

Disappointed Heart

thîi phûeng thaang jai   ที่พึ่งทางใจ

Friends often provide a shoulder to cry on, and this heart phrase means one friend has opened the disappointment of his or her heart to a close friend. The person with the "disappointed heart" finds a confessor for the dispiriting feelings. The friend is able to help the "disappointed hearted" person rid him or herself from their disappointment. The confessor is not limited to friends in the traditional sense and may include their mother or father, or a monk, or teacher—someone the person with a "disappoined heart" trusts with dispensing advice on dealing with the disappointment.

Do It Your Own Way

tham taam jai chÔOp   ทำตามใจชอบ

A person with a "do it your own way" heart is not someone who makes a good friend. Such a person who exhibits such behavior is the ultimate bore and, even worse, does not know *kreeng jai*. The elements of conduct display selfishness, insensitivity and absence of concern about the wellbeing of another. Such people, if invited into another's house, will immediately head for the kitchen, open the fridge and help themselves, then pop open a two-thousand-baht imported bottle of wine and drink it straight from the bottle as they go into your sitting room and put on a heavy- metal record with the volume turned up.

Friendly Heart

mít tra jìt mít tra jai   มิตรจิตมิตรใจ

When those around a person have a friendly and outgoing disposition, then he or she will feel they have *mít tra jìt mít tra jai*. "Friendly heart" is a sense of security that arises from the feeling of having people one can count on to be supportive. With these people one feels that a close emotional bond has been created. Such friends preclude a hostile environment and a person can let their guard down and relax. This is a long phrase and can be shortened to *mít tra jìt*. This version is more frequently used in the context of commenting on the "friendly heart" which your friend has beating in his or heart chest.

Good Friend Heart

phûean rûam jai   เพื่อนร่วมใจ

This heart phrase means that another person is your close and good friend, someone in whom you can trust and confide. A wife feels this about her husband, and he feels it about her. There is no residual fear in the heart when in the presence of this person. Instead, there is a sense of relaxation that comes from not worrying about the mask that is worn in public with strangers. One may wish to introduce a friend to a third party with "good friend heart" which is all the explanation necessary to define the nature of the relationship.

Knowledge/Cooperation Heart

rúu hěn pen jai   รู้เห็นเป็นใจ

This heart phrase is similar to *pen jai* with the added element that the person with *rúu hěn pen jai* has knowledge of and agrees to the conspiracy to do something morally suspect or illegal. While *pen jai* deals with implicit, indirect involvement; *rúu hěn pen jai* is active, knowing participation in the scheme.

Laughter in Heart

hǔa rÓ nay jai   หัวเราะในใจ

Friends can be a source of amusement. Especially when they do something that makes them appear unintentionally vulnerable, childlike. Observing such an action causes one to feel amused inside. "Laughter in the heart" may arise when a friend is diverted; perhaps he or she is lost in a daydream, and he or she trips and nearly falls, but the observing friend resists laughing out loud—which might cause the person suffering the near pratfall to lose face—but inside the friend is laughing.

Nudge Heart

sà kìt jai   สะกิดใจ

A person with a "nudge heart" has a sixth sense about people, events, and situations. This instinct is highly developed in some individuals and they are said to have then a *sà kìt jai* nature. A private investigator should have *sà kìt jai* like Sherlock Holmes who could deduce the murderer from the fact that the dog didn't bark at the time of the crime. It is a built-in emotional barometer which allows one to pick up from a gesture, a facial expression, or an article of clothing a certain tone, intention, or motive. Such a sensitive individual looks behind what most people overlook or ignore and can predict what really happened or what the outcome should be. It is not a bad quality in a stockbroker, lawyer, or bartender. A lover who is *sà kìt jai* will quickly sense if her or his other half has been unfaithful from a glance, expression or look. From such a person one cannot hide and the only chance may be to run.

Pair Heart

khûu jai   คู่ใจ

A precondition to experiencing a "pair heart" is to understand and trust another person—it may be a friend, your child, spouse or lover—then that person is your *khûu jai*. One feels joined together with another person. The union is cemented with trust. The two people involved feel a match has been made between them. The heart phrase appears frequently in the context of a friend or someone who is trusted.

Put Faith in Heart

waang jai   วางใจ

This heart phrase describes a state of being which is both positive and sought after. A person who feels *waang jai* achieves this feeling of comfort and ease in the presence of a select group of special people. He or she is able to relax with a few close friends, spouse, or lover. In this state of "put faith in heart", a person allows the public to mask fall from their face—they take off the disguise and public persona, and their true self emerges in a natural state of being. When a person feels *waang jai,* he or she feels released from the general obligation of presenting a certain face (including the strict demands of the "awe heart" state) to the outside world.

Speechless Heart

àt ân tan jai   อัดอั้นตันใจ

Friendship is about secret sharing and secret keeping. When someone has done a wrongful act and confides in his or her friend, he or she may ask the friend not to tell anyone else. The friend swears to maintain secrecy. The "speechless in the heart" is about keeping anothers confidences. The oath of secrecy makes the person taking it feel "speechless in the heart". This may be a bad feeling because the confidence keeper has the secret locked inside, with no way to let it out without violating the oath of secrecy.

United Heart

rûam jai   ร่วมใจ

samŏe jai   เสมอใจ

The "united heart" signifies a personal bond or connection with another. The feeling associated with such a connection is a hallmark of friendship. The emotional bond arises through a unity of purpose and feeling. Such feelings may arise out of friendship. The emotional state may also arise amongst co-workers who work closely together to finish a common project.

Worry Heart

klûm jai   กลุ้มใจ

The person with a "worry heart" feels sad over upon learning that his best friend has lost his job or his sweetheart. Such a person feels *klûm jai* for their friend's loss and misery. The "worry heart" offers a shoulder for another to cry on. The essence of this heart phrase is the worried condition felt about the plight of another who is usually a close friend (and perhaps yourself) when something has gone wrong or some misfortune has entered the friend's life.

Hurt Feelings
Hurt Feeling Heart

krà thuean jai   กระเทือนใจ

sà thuean jai   สะเทือนใจ

These two heart phrases apply to the classic case where another's feelings have been hurt by actions or words. Hurt feelings can also translate, in some instances (but not all) as a loss of face. One friend learns that someone she or he thought was a close friend has started a false rumor about her or his state of health. Upon learning of this betrayal, the person would experience a "hurt feeling heart". When a student is caught red-handed in the act of cheating during an examination and exposed before the entire class, the loss of face may be sufficient to cause the student to kill himself or herself by jumping off a building. Further the story of such a death or similar tragic story of suffering and hardship is also *sà thuean jai* for the reader, i.e., deeply moving. Reading a story about poor children upcountry who have not shoes or enough food to eat is also *sà thuean jai.*

Vindicated Heart

Satisfy One's Heart

sà jai   สะใจ

săa kâE jai   สาแก่ใจ

sà jai is used when someone has received their just desserts. They have done something wrong, and the time comes to pay their dues. The notion of justice behind this phrase is karmic justice. The English equivalent would be the phrase: What goes around comes around. One has promised their secretary a raise, and then later he or she breaks the promise. A week later the employer loses a big contract with a customer. Your secretary may think to herself about the boss: *sà jai*. If she said it to the boss, she might be dismissed. *säa kâE jai* is a variation of *sà jai*. If one desires to use a heart phrase which has the essence that someone else got what was coming to them, *sà jai* is the perfect choice. There is a strong sense of personal vindication in this phrase; that bad, unjust, or wrong acts have their payback in kind somewhere down the road. And when that payback day comes those hurt by the bad, unjust, or wrong experience their feeling of vindication.

Buried In the Heart

făng yùu nay hŭa jai   ฝังอยู่ในหัวใจ

făng jai   ฝังใจ

When you are a child you may have heard many stories and witnessed many incidents in the company of your family. You store them away as memories. The stories or incidents become buried in your heart and later in your life something or someone causes you to remember what was laid down when you were a child. Or the memory might be associated with your romance at school. In later life incidents of that early relationship are triggered by things said and done by your current spouse or lover. The memory of the past is *făng yùu nay hŭa jai*.

Staying in the Heart

tìt trueng jai   ติดตรึงใจ

This heart phrase is confined mainly to the written word. It has a similar meaning to *fàng jai*. The main difference is that *tìt trueng jai* describes a memory that is pleasant and happy. One goes on a holiday to Phuket and experiences the good beaches, seafood, and comfortable hotel accommodation. Later one would recall these experiences with a sense of wellness or happiness.

Obedience

Obeying the Host's Heart

long ruea taam jai pÉ   ลงเรือตามใจแป๊ะ

The basic principle is that once you get on another person's boat you follow the orders of the owner of the boat. This heart phrase is appropriate for use in connection with a person's office, house, car, boat, motorcycle (not to mention airplane, water buffalo or other forms of transportation). For instance, Lek who is from upcountry, goes to school in Bangkok and lives in a house owned by a friend of Lek's mother. The mother's friend enforces a curfew rule that Lek must return each day no later than 9.00 p.m. Lek *long ruuea taam jai pÉ* by returning to the house before 9.00 p.m. In so doing Lek is following the "boat owner's" rule.

Persuasion

Convinced Heart

yîng nÊE jai   ยิ่งแน่ใจ

One person suspects another of an act of betrayal. For instance, cash has gone missing from one's wallet. The suspected thief might be a servant, a spouse, or a child. A trap is laid and the thief is discovered to be the wallet owner's minor wife. The victim is likely to feel *yîng nÊE jai* that it was she who had lightened his wallet. The circumstances of the act does not always need to be this extreme to invoke hurt feelings, disillusionment or disappointment. A friend may have promised to deliver an important document at an appointed hour but through an act of carelessness loses the document and then avoids the person who is waiting for delivery. Once the facts are discovered, the feeling of *yîng nÊE jai* may well arise.

Persuade Heart

chák juung jai ชักจูงใจ

chák juung jai is to persuade someone to do something another person desires to be done. One may tug at the heart of the person one wishes to convince to do something or take a certain course of action. The object of "persuade heart" is to compel another person to act according to one's desire. One person or object may make another person feel *thùuk chák juung jai*. The beautiful flower in the market stall persuades someone to buy it. The attractive art cover on a book convinces another to buy the book. Or the lovely salesgirl in the department store persuades a young man to buy another telephone.

Persuade Heart

juung jai จูงใจ

When someone feels emotionally convinced about a thing, an object, or a place by reading or listening to someone else's explanations of its pleasures or virtues. If the story is amusing, then *juung jai* conveys the feelings of humor the person feels. If the story is sad, then it likewise conveys the sense of that person's feeling of sadness. The heart phrase picks up the tone from the experience of the observer or reader, persuading the heart with humor or sadness.

Negotiate Heart

pràp khwaam khâw jai ปรับความเข้าใจ

In the Thai language, one negotiates from and through the heart. This heart phrase is used as a verb: To *pràp khwaam khâw jai* is to negotiate a new understanding. There may be a misunderstanding between parties to a business arrangement, and through the process of negotiation such misunderstandings are eliminated. The "negotiate heart" is not limited to commercial deals and applies equally between lovers, friends, colleagues and classmates.

Pride

In Western literature pride and proud sometimes carry a negative implication as in Thomas Campbell's *Pleasures of Hope*, "The proud, the cold untroubled heart of stone, that never mused on sorrow but its own." In the heart phrases that follow, there are several ways to express the high opinion a person has formed of him or herself. In most instances, the source of pride is from having accomplished something of value or otherwise to have performed successfully. Pride can also be strongly felt about one's village, province or country.

Delighted Heart

plûuem jai	ปลื้มใจ
prìm jai	ปริ่มใจ
plàap plûuem jai	ปลาบปลื้มใจ

When you receive a promotion in your work and you feel proud of yourself, then you may be *plûuem jai*. This is the sense of individual accomplishment that comes from your own personal efforts. You have set out to accomplish a task and actually do so. This is a sense of pride of accomplishment. Also, it can be the transitory feeling of pride which comes from the praise or flattery given by another.

Proud Heart

phuum jai	ภูมิใจ

A person is *phuum jai* or is proud when they have accomplished something that makes them feel good or successful. They can feel ten feet tall with a sense of accomplishment. A person can feel proud about themselves or others; and others may have a sense of pride in you. Or a "proud heart" may come from feeling part of a larger organization of people: a feeling of pride towards one's country, hometown, university, or family.

Strength Heart

kamlang jai	กำลังใจ
phalang jai	พลังใจ

A person who feels a sense of accomplishment or success possesses *kamlang jai*. The girl who wins a beauty contest or the football player who does well in a game also has *kamlang jai*. Tiger Woods no doubt has such a heart after winning a major golf tournment. After an argument, when one person apologizes, then one or both people involved will have *kamlang jai*.

Responsibility & the Family

There are exceptions to every rule, but generally the family occupies a central role in the lives of most Thais. There is an abiding sense of obligation to the family within each member. Traditionally, children were raised to feel responsible to their parents throughout their lives. An obligation of such dimensions that it could never be fully paid. Many of the phrases below are expressions which often occur in a family context, although they may be used outside the family as well.

Attentive Heart

aw jai sày   เอาใจใส่

This is another heart phrase which has the same basic meaning as *sày jai*. One demonstrates their interest in another person's welfare and happiness, and advises them on the best course of action in accomplishing what will be in their best interest. When the advisor is a person of a higher social rank or senior in age, then such advice is rendered within the context of "awe heart". Here is an example where the "interested heart" advice giver meets with the "awe hearted" advice receiver. In such circumstances, it may be difficult for the receiver not to accept the advice.

Bear in Mind Heart

sày jai   ใส่ใจ

A mother is *sày jai* by reminding her sons and daughters of the importance of an education. By doing so, the mother demonstrates an interest in the future welfare of her children. In other relationships, the "bear in mind heart" is a demonstration of one person's wish to guide another person's future, whether a child, lover, spouse or friend, in a positive, helpful way. Such a person wishes for what is best for them and encourages others in their lives. His or her action and involvement in the process of encouragement, guidance and direction is *sày jai*.

Center Heart

jai klaang   ใจกลาง

The heart phrase is, among other things, descriptive of the location of a building or street. For example, some would say that Siam Square is *jai klaang* in Bangkok, "in the heart of" town. Others might vote for Silom Road. "Center heart" also has another meaning, for the feelings one may have about the importance of another person in their life. The mother or father might be thought of as *jai klaang* for a child. Though the more common phrase would be *sǔun klaang* ส่วนกลาง as an expression that the child represents the center of her or his family. Parents occupy a central place in the hearts of their children.

Force Heart

fǔuen jai   ฝืนใจ

The "force" comes from the outside in this case. Someone is forced by another or by circumstances to do something they would rather avoid. The "force" is requesting (or requiring) someone to fulfill an obligation. For instance, Lek dislikes a particular customer of the company but her boss requests that Lek take this client to dinner. This is important for the company. Lek complies with her boss' request but feels *fǔuen jai*. Another example is the person who has lost their job in the financial sector and is "forced" by economic circumstances to accept employment in the night time entertainment sector.

Forced Heart

khǔuen jai   ขืนใจ

The nature and emotional anguish of the force is significantly more profound in the context of *khǔuen jai*. Many times this heart phrase is used to describe the emotional state of a woman who has been sexually forced or violated. This horrible crime leaves a deep scar on the woman's heart. There are other circumstances, how ever, where *khǔuen jai* is used to denote an exterior force compelling someone to act against their will. For example, Lek has been seeing Vinai for eighteen months and they have a serious relationship. Only Vinai is a noodle vendor and Lek's parents disapprove of her relationship with him. The parents "force" Lek to marry a man chosen by them. She does not love this man. Lek feels *khǔuen jai* in carrying out the obligations she feels that is owed to parents by marrying a man of their choice and abandoning the man she loves.

Heavy Heart

nàk jai   หนักใจ

When someone feels responsible for and worries about their children, parents, spouse or lover, then you feel *nàk jai* towards that person. They may have a son who does not live a good and respectable life; he refuses to work, hangs out at nightclubs with questionable friends, and otherwise has a lifestyle far below your expectations. Then they will likely experience firsthand a "heavy heart."

Interested Heart

sǒn jai   สนใจ

This heart phrase is a common one in Thai, and indicates that one person is interested in another person, thing, or activity. The level of interest may be small. A vendor may use the term as an indirect way of selling you goods. Sometimes the heart phrase is used to determine whether a person has a preference. Other times, the heart phrase may be posed in question form: Are you interested in going to the movies? Are you interested in an article written about the stock market?

Keenly Interested Heart

fày jai   ใฝ่ใจ

While *sǒn jai* is an expression of interest in someone or a thing, *fày jai* combines intention with the element of action. A person is not only interested in golf but plays the game. At work the project assigned to someone is something they are interested in and are actively involved in realizing. A person's friends will see that they are *fày jai* when a his or her intention and actions coincide, whether it is a sport, hobby, education or work.

Single-minded Heart

jai jòt jai jOO   ใจจดใจจ่อ

Someone has devoted themselves to a project such as learning Thai. They take the study seriously and spend considerable time and effort, leaving other things in their life in the background. At this point that person would be said to have *jai jòt jai jOO*. This may be translated into a kind of self-responsibility.

A "single-minded heart" can have a dark side as well. The object of another's desire which they possess *jai jòt jai jOO* might not be what someone wants for themselves. For example, someone's spouse may intend to invest the family's life savings in mining company stock based upon a rumour of gold being discovered. She or he is *jai jòt jai jOO* about such an investment, while other family members would rather keep the family investment in a saving account.

Unwilling Heart

jam jai   จำใจ

The feeling of a "unwilling heart" comes from carrying out one's responsibility even though one might wish they were doing something else or were someplace else. The "unwillingness" comes from inside the person rather than from outside pressure. The obligations is fulfilled but begrudgingly. Such a person would rather be with their friends rather than taking their mother shopping or to the temple. They would rather be sleeping at eight in the morning, but must be at the office working by tht time. So they pull themselves out of bed and do what has to be done: Go to work. One can *jam jai* themselves in these obligations and tasks. One does one's duty.

Surprise

As a general rule, to surprise another in Thai culture is not welcomed. In public, where the mask and costume are worn, and the interactions carefully scripted for the social situation, a surprise can cause confusion and discontent. By its very nature, a surprise is outside of the script, beyond what is expected. Amongst friends a surprise is one thing, but in a formal setting of strangers, to surprise another should be avoided.

Alarm Heart

tùuen trà nòk tòk jai   (ตื่น) ตระหนกตกใจ

As the world collapses around one the emotional spasm is one of alarm. In this heart wake-up call, the person is submerged in difficult times and feels panic. There is upheaval which leaves the person helpless and not knowing which way to turn. They pick up the newspaper and see the stock market has fallen twenty-five percent overnight and they are *trà nòk tòk jai.* They go to the office and discover their building has burned down, or they go to their tailor and learn he has increased his prices by one hundred percent. In each case, a person who is *trà nòk tòk jai* is responding with alarm to a situation.

Amazed Heart

plâEk jai   แปลกใจ

The meaning is similar to *pra làat jai. plâEk jai* is slightly less formal; and though used in spoken or written Thai, it is most often an oral expression. There is a sense of strangeness or weirdness in an event or a person's action that brings on the condition of the "amazed heart." The key component is the element of the unexpected. A person sees their desk partners from fourth grade, someone he or she hasn't seen in thirty years, walking down Sukhumvit Road with an ex-spouse would likely feel *plâEk jai.*

Exclamation Mark Heart

khrûeang mǎay tòk jai   เครื่องหมายตกใจ

khrûeang mäay tòk jai means the exclamation point used in writing. It is used to signify an exclamatory sentence—which is a kind of a written sign posted to announce the writer intended an effect like a surprise.

Fallen Heart

tòk jai   ตกใจ
tòk òk tòk jai   ตกอกตกใจ
sà dûng jai   สะดุ้งใจ

A heart might be said to fall when someone sneaks into the shower and frightens their lover. He or she will no doubt feel *tòk jai*. This is a feeling of one's pulse beating in one's throat, the terrifying sense of being in sudden danger. The act of making someone scared out of their wits is *tham hây tòk jai*. *sà dûng jai* is appropriate for use in a poem.

Panic Heart

jai túm túm tôOm tôOm   ใจตุ๋มตุ๋มต้อมต้อม

This heart phrase anticipates an emotional state arising out of a sense of danger or uncertainty. He or she has run a red light and a policeman pulls him or her over. As the policeman approaches the car to issue a ticket, they may feel a sense of panic. Or someone is alone in their house reading and they hear glass breaking in an empty bedroom. It's likely their heart is racing in their chest, and they experience the physical sensation associated with terror or fear.

Stunned Heart

jai hǎay jai khwâm   ใจหายใจคว่ำ

This is another example of a nasty surprise or turn of events lurking out there. Suddenly one turns a corner, and finds themselves in a burning hotel with the fire doors locked or in the middle of a street riot or in a major road accident. The feeling is one of being stunned. *jai häay jai khwâm* is akin to a significant jolt, an emotional shock rolls over the person experiencing it. The literal translation is "heart lost, heart overturned." This sense of loss and overturning of the heart arises from a near-miss with disaster, violence, or the trauma resulting from a brush with death experience.

Surprised Heart

prà làat jai   ประหลาดใจ

You feel *prà làat jai* when someone acts out of character, or when one confronts a situation which is not expected. It corresponds to feelings associated with suspicion or doubt which comes when the feeling that you expected is not what you received. It is a versatile heart phrase that can be employed in many situations. For instance, it can be used to express feelings about the weather or the environment. Looking at a dirty, polluted *klong* and feeling *pra làat jai*. The "surprised heart" can also occur during a long spell in heavy Bangkok traffic: An uneasy feeling develops as people are confined for hours inside a car or bus. Or as the value of the Thai baht nosedives to an all time low, the feelings of doubt cause a "surprised heart" among many millions of people.

Heart Talk
Warfare

Chapter 7

Heart talk provides a rich arsenal of phrases for emotional warfare. There are certain heart phrases which signal a warning that the speaker may erupt into violence, or if said to another person might, given the circumstances, provoke a fight. When verbal war breaks out, the Thai language provides an arsenal of powerful phrases to attack another person's heart. Make no mistake about it, these phrases are like smart bombs which can find and destroy their target. But smart verbal bombs must be used by smart people and in the right circumstances to avoid heavy emotional fallout.

Many of these heart words are fighting words when addressed to a Thai speaker. They would be interpreted as a personal insult; some rank as character assassination *par excellence*. And most people do not take kindly to personal insults from others. Even the most tolerate and patient Thai would be provoked to anger with many of these phrases, so they should be used with considerable discretion.

You want to pick a fight in Thai? The oral weapon is an attack on the other person's heart. The words are to be used with extreme caution. They are not "joking around" phrases. Anyone wishing such a conflict should think twice, then again, and if they still are determined, they ought to do themselves a favor and make a trip to the airport and find another language.

After you have been in a verbal fire-fight (and survived), and wish to make up for damage inflicted, then once again you return to phrases of the heart. What you have attacked—the heart of the other—is what must be healed. When the moment arises to express regret for resorting to the use of heavy weapons of the heart, then you can turn to the end of Chapter 7 and find expressions of sorrow.

Battle Cries
Astringent and Bitter Heart

jai fàat jai khŏm　ใจฝาดใจขม

When a woman has broken her lover's heart, the lover will likely feel *jai faàt jai khŏm;* experience an astringent and bitter feeling inside. This becomes the "sharp knife time" in the relationship, when the twist of the emotional knife is the most painful. It is time to turn and run as fast as one can before the "astringent and bitter hearted" person, along with assorted friends, and family members take their revenge. The heart phrase is slightly dated and now it would be more likely to hear the expression *khŏm khùuen jai.*

Cut Heart

bàat măang jai　บาดหมางใจ

măang jai　หมางใจ

rá khaang jai　ระคางใจ

When someone has a quarrel with their friend and a week later see the friend on the street, they may feel *măang jai.* One may wish to avoid those they have had a conflict or quarrel with. Seeing one's former lover coming down the street, he or she may duck around a corner to avoid talking with ex-lover. A person feels *măang jai* about dealing with the old flame and wishes to escape the feelings he or she evokes by making a retreat in the opposite direction.

Grudge Heart

phìt jai kan　ผิดใจกัน

phìt jai　ผิดใจ

Someone has had a run-in with another and they feel upset or sore as a result of the encounter. It may have been an argument, or he or she double-crossed another, or the feeling may result from a lingering sense of being wronged. Someone has accumulated a grudge. They will likely feel *phìt jai kan.* This is a low grade grudge and unhappiness. Such a feeling is written across the actions and words of a person harboring "grudge heart". It is good advice to avoid a person who generates such a feeling. At the same time, it is likely such feelings are transitory and will pass, and will not create a permanent rift in the relationship.

Hot Heart

jai rÓOn ใจร้อน

In the context of warfare terms, the phrase describes a person who feels anger with another. The experience of such anger is to enter the state of being *jai rÓOn*. Or *jai rÓOn* feelings may arise from the pressure of work, traffic jams, being stood up for an appointment or date, or similar obstacles that prevent one from realizing their goal, doing what they want, going where they wish, or otherwise frustrating raised expectations. In the extreme case of *jai rÓOn* the person may resort to violent language or action; this results from the sudden loss of one's temper. The "hot hearted" may be a personality type as well. Someone who has a hair-trigger temper and easily explodes whenever another does not perform as desired.

Moody Heart

khîi ngùt ngìt (jai) ขี้หงุดหงิด (ใจ)

The Thai word *khîi* in this context translates as "excessive". The literal translation is excrement. This is a commonly used (and heard) heart phrase. It means someone is acting moody or is indeed the moody type. The "moody hearted" person is easily upset with small, minor things. People, kids, dogs all get on their nerves. Such a personality type is not largely favored because it comes along with complaints about treatment or decisions made by others. This phrase is often used by couples, with one accusing the other of having a "moody heart". The chances are good that someone referred to as *khîi ngùt ngìt jai* will not take this as a compliment.

Pain Heart

jèp jai เจ็บใจ
jèp krà dOOng jai เจ็บกระดองใจ

When the husband or wife finds that their spouse has a lover he or she will be *jèp jai*. The feeling of *jèp jai* is an extreme, highly volatile state which may precede violent action. The husband or wife may try to kill the offending spouse and/or his or her lover. It is one rung down the ladder of the emotional violence scale from *jai fàat jai khǒm*. It has been known to come packaged with fists and weapons.

Regrets

At the end of a fight or confrontation most people (sooner or later) have the desire to make up. To make amends. To put the relationship back on a civil basis. How one makes up in the Thai language depends on whether the problem was with a stranger, a lover, a best friend, or a child. Nevertheless, one will need access to the stock of appropriate metaphors included below.

Feel Sorry Heart

rúu sùek sěa jai   รู้สึกเสียใจ

"Feel sorry heart" is a heart expression for sorrow. Something has happened to make one sorry. There may have been an accident for which they feel responsible. Or maybe someone's best friend or family member has become seriously ill. They feel sorrow. This is a more formal heart expression of sorrow than "lose heart".

Lose Heart

sěa jai   เสียใจ

When someone wishes to express that they are sorry in Thai, then *sěa jai* is the right verbal phrase to cover most cases. Another way of conveying the same feeling of regret for an act or word is the adjective form *nâa sěa jai* which means the same as *sěa jai*. The noun version of *sěa jai*, or in English "sorrow", is *khwaam sěa jai*. Another useful expression is *sěa jai dûay ná* or "Please accept my sympathy" or "I am sorry that something unfortunate has happened to you."

This heart phrase is frequently used, including the untimely death of a person one's knows. Sorrow may be felt about the suffering of others. The loss of a job or the declining economy.

Lose Chest, Lose Heart

sěa òk sěa jai   เสียอกเสียใจ

One is feeling very sad when using this heart phrase. It means a kind of personal sorrow is being experienced. It is a slang expression and is less commonly used than *sěa jai*.

Return Heart

klàp jai   กลับใจ

To repent for what one has done to wrong another is *klàp jai*. Repentance is a return of the heart. The heart phrase might appear where a criminal testifies against gang members but the motive is more to help himself than to repent for what he has done. There is also an element of redemption. The person may wish to become a good person, and his change of intention or plans may be evidence of *klàp jai*. The emotional content is one's acceptance of responsibility for a wrong or harm caused to another, and implicit is the message that the person causing the harm will not do it again.

Revenge

Revenge Heart

jai aakhâat mâat ráay   ใจอาฆาตมาดร้าย

Hearing this heart phrase from a Thai speaker standing next to you at the bar, and you are the object of this address, then having a bulletproof vest is strongly recommended. Otherwise, a quick exit from the bar is the next best option. "Revenge heart" is an-eye-for-an-eye, tooth-for-a-tooth kind of heart talk. This is an adjective to describe a person who is unforgiving and will never forget the pain or insult and in the end will take revenge. It is the verbal warning that revenge will follow. Anyone described as *jai aakhâat mâat ráay* is someone to fear and avoid: and if the revenge is directed toward another, then they may soon be on their way to the next life.

Revenge Heart

khÉEn jai   แค้นใจ

Revenge happens for many different reasons. In the public arena, in the heat of politics, one faction of a political party may take revenge for the dumping of one of their members from the Cabinet by withdrawing their support and voting with the opposition to cause the government to fall. A person who cheats, fails to pay their debts, or causes disgrace to another's name may awake one morning to find a severed dog's head inside the family compound or his or her car spray-painted or otherwise damaged. On a personal level, should one find that their spouse has been unfaithful, the revenge may take the a number of forms; from clothes being torn, cutting of certain body parts of the unfaithful person, or sleeping with another person.

Revenge Heart

phùuk jai jèp ผูกใจเจ็บ

If one intends to cause another harm or injury, the forming of the intention is *phùuk jai jèp*. Panit's husband is unfaithful and she discovers evidence of his infidelity. She decides to remove a very important organ from her husband's body as he sleeps. Panit's intention to carry out this act of revenge is *phùuk jai jèp*. Another illustration comes from politics. In the past, it has been reported that during an election, if a person has been given money by a candidate to distribute to voters but keeps the money himself, and that candidate loses the election and discovers the theft, then the candidate may form the intention to cause harm to the dishonest canvasser (though the dishonesty of the canvasser must be viewed with some irony given his or her mission). The planning of this revenge is *phùuk jai jèp*.

Verbal Weapons

These heart phrases are for the truly wicked. That is the brutal, evil, savage and bad individuals who cause pain and destruction to others. The cruel and heartless individual normally acts in utter disregard for the feelings of others. In the extreme case, such an individual behavior involves rape, murder and mayhem. As linguistic weapons, such heart phrases should be used with caution.

Animal Heart

jai sàt ใจสัตว์

You don't want to say this in a crowded bar unless you are with a body builder who is packing a 9mm with a full clip. This is guaranteed to wipe the smile off anyone's face.

"Animal heart" is a noun. It is something one possesses as a personality attribute. But it is a word to be used with extreme caution; it is a fighting word, and one that may accelerate a verbal battle to physical blows being exchanged. For example, a murderer would be thought to possess *jai sàt*. The Chinese cannibal who ate Thai children after World War II is the quintessential *jai sàt* of Thai folklore. In Thai *jai sàt* is a horrible insult to another person. You are saying that person is like an animal.

Bad Heart

jai leew saam ใจเลวทราม

"Bad heart" is hurled at someone who is thought to be bad or evil. The heart phrase is reserved for villains. Such a bad person is felt to have an evil heart, a heart without feeling for the plight of others. Because the heart is bad, this person with *jai leew saam* may inflict pain on others.

Brutal Heart

jai juùet jai dam ใจจืดใจดำ

One should add "brutal heart" to the growing list of insults. It means, like *jai bàap*, this person is no good, a bully, a thug, and a danger to others, and those are his better qualities. "Brutal heart" is one more heart phrase, if used indiscriminately with strangers, could lead to a period of hospitalization.

Cruel Heart

jai am mahìt ใจอำมหิต

Someone has inflicted some major damage to property or another person before they hear a Thai say that they have *jai am mahìt*. Such a person is a heavy hitter of death and destruction; and uses violence like everyday cologne. Pol Pot, the infamous leader of the Khmer Rouge, provided during his life a local example in neighboring Cambodia. In less dramatic circumstances, the person who beats their maid, spouse or children is also a candidate for the label of "cruel heart."

Evil Heart

jai tàm cháa ใจต่ำช้า

The person with *jai tàm cháa* is more than simply cruel by nature. He or she is touched with the brush of evil. The most extreme examples are those officials who gave the orders to operate the gas chambers and those who carried out those orders under the Nazi regime during World War II.

A military commander who orders landmines to be placed in an area with a high concentration of civilians knowing that the mines will inflict a large number of casualties would have *jai tàm cháa*.

The factory owner who keeps his young employees in a virtual state of imprisonment. The employees cannot leave the premises, the owner gives them only a small amount of rice each day, and forces them to work eighteen hours a day, and beats them if they complain, attempt to run away or fall asleep on the job.

Face of Deer, Heart of Tiger

nâa núea jai sǔea   หน้าเนื้อใจเสือ

This is an ancient Thai proverb which is similar to "a wolf in sheep's clothing." One does not go around saying this heart phrase to another Thai speaker unless their life insurance is fully paid. It is a close cousin to *jai sàt*. The English translation makes it sound harmless, childlike. If you try this one, the chances are you will get yourself a quick kick-boxing lesson.

Giant Heart

jai yák   ใจยักษ์

jai yák jai maan   ใจยักษ์ใจมาร

Another insult guaranteed to provoke anger and possibly a hostile reaction is to suggest that another person has *jai yák*. The metaphor of a giant carries an extremely negative image. In this context, a giant is not looked upon as a large, friendly person, but as a mean, cruel, and brutal monster-like figure of a child's nightmares. Such a "giant hearted" person is without humanity and without normal feelings. Like "bad heart", the heart phrase is used to express revulsion about those who show little true feeling about the wellbeing of others.

Low Heart

jai tàm saam   ใจต่ำทราม

A person who is *jai tàm saam* is about as bad as a person can get and still be considered a member of the human race. He or she may have thrown his or her daughters in the street or sold them into prostitution. He or she may have killed their parents, landmined Sukhumvit Road, and barbecued local *soi* dogs. The kind of evil, dangerous, and horrible person has a number of heart phrases to describe him.

Many Heart

lǎay jai   หลายใจ

"Many heart" is often used as a bad news metaphor. Often speculation over who has an "outside heart" and "second heart" is the subject of gossip or small talk. A person who is *lǎay jai* cannot (or will not) be faithful to another person. While it can also refer to someone who has a number of interests or hobbies, a foreigner has to use caution to ensure from the context, gestures and tone that the phrase was intended to apply to relationships. If a person has been called *lǎay jai*, it likely means they are viewed as someone who has collected multiple lovers. Sometimes the English word "butterfly" is used by Thai speakers to identify the "many hearted" person.

Perverted Heart

jai saam   ใจทราม

"Perverted heart" is in the same class and character as *jai tàm* — an evil, very bad person. Such a person may exploit child labour in a factory. The factory boss may refuse to pay the workers. It may used interchangeably with *jai tàm*. It is possible to combine the words and say *jai tàm saam*.

The heart phrase is normally applied to a person who indulges in perverted activity. Perversion in this case has an immoral quality attached. The man who fondles women on a bus has *jai saam*, and if is caught by the authorities might well spend some time learning heart phrases inside a Thai jail. The heart phrase can apply to both genders. A woman who in a fit of rage who throws boiling water on the legs of a crying child would also be said to have a "perverted heart."

Savage Heart

jai thamin   ใจทมิฬ

A person who possesses a "savage heart" has a large capacity for brutality. Included in this category would be those who commit international war crimes such as genocide. Such people often resort to the murder of innocent women and children in a civil war. On a more limited scale of action, *jai thamin* also may be used to describe a professional gunman who kills others for money.

Heart Talk
Body Talk

Chapter 8

A number of heart phrases are not directly connected with emotions or the metaphysics of emotions, but these expressions describe physical conditions. How the body functions (or malfunctions) has a special vocabulary. An emotionally stressed situation may bring on the physical conditions described below. These heart phrases communicates the nature of how the body reacts to stress, disease, surprise, nerves, excitement or fear. One can select among the heart phrases in this chapter to describe body smells and heart attacks, and a variety of descriptions for breathing and trembling. The language that expresses the physical act of dying and the feelings associated with dying are also found in this chapter.

Hand Heart

jai mue   ใจมือ

jai muue has two different meanings. First is an ancient unit of measurement. Four standard palmfuls (*jai muue*) equals one fistful (*kum muue*). This measurement was used for rice or salt when there was other way of measuring the units to be sold. The second meaning of *jai muee* is the center of the palm of the hand.

Head Heart

hŭa jai   หัวใจ

Moving from the heart as the centre of feelings, this heart phrase allows one to enter the realm of biology. *hŭa jai* is the organ known as the heart located inside a person's chest cavity and is assigned the task of pumping blood twenty-four hours a day to the rest of the body.

Breathing, passing out, and smells are covered by a number of heart expressions.

Breath Heart

lom hǎay jai   ลมหายใจ

This heart phrase relates to one's actual breath. The air that goes in and out of the nostrils and into the lungs is *lom hǎay jai*.

Breathe Freely Heart

hǎay jai khlÔOng   หายใจคล่อง

This is ordinary, normal, unobstructed breathing. If someone has a bad head cold then they cannot *hǎay jai khlÔOng*. "Breathe freely heart" is also a metaphor for being able to breathe easily when everything is going according to plan. When there are no serious problems or obstacles in daily life, this is the normal condition.

Breathing Heart

hǎay jai   หายใจ

The verb *hǎay jai* is the Thai expression which means the act of breathing. There are also romantic notions which are a variation of this phrase, such as *thúk lom hǎay jai* which means to think of someone with every breath taken, or to think of someone all the time.

Breathing Through the Mouth Heart

hǎay jai thaang pàak   หายใจทางปาก

A person who is a mouth-breather might hear someone using this heart phrase to describe their way of breathing.

Cannot Breathe Heart

hǎay jai mây ÒOk   หายใจไม่ออก

A person who cannot breathe will feel *hǎay jai mây ÒOk*. This is obviously not a feeling they will experience for very long before either passing out or dying. It is also the stuffy feeling of spending a night in a hot, closed room without a fan or air conditioning. An hour in the back of a tuk-tuk on Sukhumvit Road during a traffic jam can produce the same condition.

Exhale Heart

hăay jai ÒOk   หายใจออก

When one breathes out or exhales the air from their lungs, they are *hăay jai ÒOk*. The expression (which is the complement of "inhale heart") is also a technical term mostly confined to a doctor's examination room.

Fragrant Heart

hŎOm chûuen jai   หอมชื่นใจ

Conversations about good and bad smells is often part of social conversations in Thailand. What (and who) smells bad is largely avoided, and there is a directness about voicing disapproval of bad smells. The same directness applies to good smells. The fragrance of flowers, food, and perfume, to mention only three examples is an experience that makes the heart feel better.

Hold Breath Heart

àt ân jai   อัดอั้นใจ

The expression describes a physical state of feeling dreadful. What is characteristic of this dread is the helplessness of not being able to say or do anything to alter the condition of holding one's breath.

Holding the Breath of Heart

klân jai   กลั้นใจ

It is a boiling hot midsummer day and a person walks past a polluted *klong* which is giving off a rich variety of foul, pungent odors. As they pass by the *klong*, a little wind blows the stench across their path, causing him or her to *klân jai*. They hold their breath. The heart phrase applies generally to some bad smell and the natural reflex action of holding your breath in reaction to the smell.

Inhale Heart

hăay jai khâw   หายใจเข้า

"Inhale heart" is the Thai verb form for breathing in or inhaling. *hăay jai khâw* is a technical term found in a medical textbooks or a phrase that a patient with a respiratory condition who goes to a hospital might expect to hear from a Thai doctor using a stethoscope as he or she performs a physical examination.

Not Convenient to Breathe Heart

hǎay jai mây sà dùak   หายใจไม่สะดวก

When someone smells a foul or rotten odor, or when they have a heavy head cold, then they feel *hǎay jai mây sà dùak*. This is the opposite of *hǎay jai khlÔOng* or breathing freely.

Suspended Breathing

hǎay jai mây thûa thÓOng   หายใจไม่ทั่วท้อง

When a person is excited or frightened their breathing rate rapidly increases, and they may experience a shortness of breath—this state of being means some excitement or nervous feeling makes it hard to breathe. Someone may have seen their lover arm-in-arm with another on Sukhumvit Road, and this unexpected sight acted like a sudden punch in the stomach; and they found themselves, among other feelings, unable to control their breathing. The rapid breathing state is not unlike hyperventilation. Someone else may have discovered that their life savings are deposited in a financial institution that has gone bankrupt. In either of these cases, the person may experience "suspended breathing".

Tight Heart

nÊEn jai   แน่นใจ

Someone feels short of breath. Maybe they cannot catch their breath. He or she may be out of shape but presses themselves to finish a ten-mile charity marathon in Lumpini Park, and as he or she pulls to a stop they feel "tight hearted" or *nÊEn jai*. The other case is someone is about to experience a heart attack.

Dying

When a person is about to die, there are some *heart phrases they* might hear being whispered in Thai by those around them. Also included here are other heart phrases for heart problems and heart attacks.

Breathe One's Lost Heart

khàat jai   ขาดใจ

Several heart expressions such as "breathe one's lost heart" translate as a person's dying breath. The first, *khàat jai,* has a poetic ring in English translation. It means the last dying breath before a person dies. The emphasis is on the physical act of taking that last breath before death.

Failure of the Heart

hǔa jai waay   หัวใจวาย

"Failure of heart" is the Thai expression for the basic garden-variety heart attack. If it is used as a noun, then the person is already dead. If it is used as a verb, then the person spoken about is suffering from a heart attack. A person who complains of *experiencing hǔa jai waay* will likely be understood to be asking for an emergency trip to the hospital.

Finished Heart

sîn jai   สิ้นใจ

Sîn jai is a verb for the act of dying. It is a euphemism like "passing away", used as a polite substitute for saying someone has died. The person who feels he is dying may use *sîn jai*. The phrase may mask a bad feeling mixed with fear and horror and sadness. The feeling is generated from the realization that a person's life is being extinguished. But a religious person such as a monk who feels *sîn jai* might have a good feeling. Unlike *khàat jai* which is the physical act of the last breath before death, *sîn jai* is the Thai phrase used to avoid using more direct words such as: Die, death, or dying.

Shriveled Heart

jai fÒO   ใจฝ่อ

Withered Heart

hǔa jai lîip   หัวใจลีบ

One meaning of the heart phrase, "withered heart" is to describe that a broken heart caused by a lover's sudden departure. The second meaning of "withered heart" is a medical opinion from a doctor breaking the unfortunate news that a person has heart disease. *jai fÒO* is used in the same context as *hǔa jai lîip*.

Heart Disease

rôok hǔa jai   โรคหัวใจ

This is a medical term to describe a physical condition of the heart. In other words, this is not a metaphor but the physical organ beating in the chest of each person. If one hears their doctor using this phrase, it is time to make certain that their will and health insurance policies are in good order.

Faint Heart

jai wǐw ใจหวิว

"Faint heart" is a physical sensation of feeling dizzy or about to faint. When someone peers down from the top of a forty-story building without safety railings, they may feel dizzy as if they might faint. At this point a friend may ask them if they are *jai wǐw*. Or someone has spent too much time sunbathing on the beach under a hot tropical sun or has checked their bar bill after entertaining a half-dozen friends at an expensive club; afterwards he or she may be *jai wǐw*. That sense of being light-headed, dizzy, giddy that are precusors to losing consciousness. Remember that monster of a roller coaster ride at the amusement park? The one that caused sheer terror as time appeared to stop. That is another way to have experienced *jai wǐw*.

Shake, Rattle and Roll

The following heart phrases are used to describe a person who is afraid, startled, nervous, or surprised, resulting in the feeling of their heart dancing inside their chest.

Dancing Heart

jai têen ใจเต้น

This is the feeling of surprise or being excited. Vinai is busily brushing his teeth alone in the bathroom. His girlfriend sneaks in behind him and he catches sight of her in the mirror. This unexpected event may cause him to feel *jai têen*, his heart dancing in his chest from the shock of seeing the unexpected.

Encourage Heart

ráw jai เร้าใจ

"Encourage heart" is a state of excitement. Another person makes them feel excited. When someone is watching two kick-boxers from a box seat, and have bet money on one boxer, but that boxer is down on points going into the last round, the punter will feel his heart dancing inside his chest. This is *ráw jai*. The bikini-clad woman walking along the beach may also have a similar effect on others sun bathing.

153
•
๑๕๓

Fast Heart Beat

hǔa jai têen rEEng　หัวใจเต้นแรง

A person who is afraid or startled feels as if their heart has jumped into their throat. In matters of the heart, the feeling is *hǔa jai têen rEEng*. The person feels the physical pulse beating in her or his chest and throat. They are on their way to a panic attack. The expression of "fast heart beat" equips one to convey this condition to others.

Shake Heart

sà thuean jai　สะเทือนใจ

The feeling of *sà thuean jai* means that a person physically feels their body tremble or shake. The cause of the trembling or shaking may be from an illness or from an emotional cause such as a confrontation with someone else. For example, the body builder at the next table has just threatened to do twenty bench presses with another patron's body before throwing him through the window. The patron will likely feel "shake heart" as a result of this threat.

Heart Talk
Self-Control

Chapter 9

Although self-control is a relatively short chapter, the feelings of restraint are contained in some of the most important heart phrases in the Thai language. In Thai culture considerable virtue is attached a person's ability to exercise restraint or control over his or her feelings of rage, anger, or upset.

The ideal, in the Thai tradition, is not to be drawn into an emotional reaction when provoked. There is an attempt to avoid confrontations and the heated exchanges. Of course this is an ideal, and anyone pushed hard and long enough will react with anger. The fighting words and words of rejection and criticism are examples of the kind of provocation one seeks to overcome with heart phrases contained in this chapter. There is a competition for the heart. In one orbit around the heart are the heart warfare phrases attacking another person; and in another orbit are the deep-seated cultural values of using restraint to deflect the attack. This contradiction is not always easy to resolve. Indeed it might be thought the need for resolution is a Western rather than a Thai notion.

The heart expressions are the first-line of emotional defense against such attacks, insults or provocation.

At the same time, self-control as embodied in these heart phrases is a broader concept than simply attempts to avoid anger. Also valued are ideals of calmness, concentration, and self-control. The cultural value is a person with a heart capable of overcoming rash action based on random impulses or being constantly distracted with the thousand daily things that compete for our attention.

Addictive Heart

tìt jai ติดใจ

An addictive heart, in essence, lacks self-control or discipline. The desire is to repeat an activity or an experience, especially one that has a strong element of excitement attached. For instance, someone may become addicted to certain sports such as golf, swimming, roller-blading, or skiing. They achieve a thrill from this activity and, in the extreme case, give up all other activities in order to pursue the one that gives them the adrenalin rush they demand.

Brief Moment Heart

ùet jai   อึดใจ

The control of the heart is for a brief time frame in the case of *ùet jai*. One is requested, or request another, to hold or wait a short period of time. The reason may be that someone is not available. Or it may be that waiting is desirable. Normally the phrase is used amongst people who are friends and not between strangers. Someone in the family may be using the telephone and another member needs to make a phone call. The one using the phone, upon hearing the request asks her or him wait a brief moment. Another reason may be to muster up the courage to endure a moment of pain. Thus a child who is frightened when given an injection may be gently assured by his mother and the attending nurse that the pain will last only a moment.

Calm Heart

rá ngáp jai   ระงับใจ

This heart phrase is a varation on *sangòp jai*. When someone blows their top and the anger flows like lava, someone may tell them to *rá ngáp jai*. That is, calm down, take a deep breath, and don't let the anger carry them away into doing some act they may later regret.

Calm Heart

sangòp jai   สงบใจ

When a person feels an unpleasant emotional upset, then they will try to *sangòp jai* or calm themselves. "Calm heart" is a state of trying to control how one feels in the midst of an emotional thunderstorm. When someone feels emotional upset—for instance, feeling either *hàk jai*, or their lover has abandoned them and they feel *jèp jai*—they may wish to take refuge in a "calm heart". A friend may suggest to another who is experiencing emotional turmoil to *sangòp jai*. It is the ability to control the hurtful or negative emotions like anger and to replace them with a sense of calmness. Assuming that one has suceeded in calming themselves at the moment of crisis they will feel *sangòp jai*.

Concentrate Heart

sǎm ruam jai   สำรวมใจ

The idea of "concentrate heart" comes from the Buddhist notion of meditation. In a Buddhist country like Thailand, this idea of meditation translates in this heart phrase as concentration. One is centered, not distracted or off balance. They are in the groove of the moment as their heart concentrates. At that time they are concentrated or *sǎm ruam jai*.

Concentrate Goodness Heart

sǎm ruam kaay waa jaa jai   สำรวมกาย วาจา ใจ

This heart phrase emphasizes the concentration on the good deed or on speaking the appropriate or kind word. To *sǎm ruam kaay waa jaa jai* is to be in the state of awareness that what is being done or being said is right and appropriate for the circumstances.

Control Heart

khòm jai   ข่มใจ
bang kháp jai   บังคับใจ

Control becomes a powerful metaphor when linked with the heart. In the face of adversity someone feels *khòm jai* when they do not become angry or sorry or react in a negative, hostile fashion toward the person who has rejected, criticized or hurt them. The person under emotional attack as a result of an insult or provocation may wish to feel *khòm jai*. Another variation of this phrase is *sàkòt jai* which also translates as control heart. When one is in the heat of an emotional response, they should try repeating *khòm jai* and *sàkòt jai* as a kind of code of conduct that Thais expect of themselves, and of others as well.

Control Heart

sàkòt jai   สะกดใจ
sàkòt òk sàkòt jai   สะกดอกสะกดใจ
hâam jai   ห้ามใจ

These three heart phrases share the same core quality of controlling one's feelings. The person who can control his or her heart will have a cool heart or *jai yen*. In heavy Bangkok motor traffic, a motorist who is stalled for fifteen minutes at an intersection because the light appears to stay red forever may initially shout and curse, but before fully losing his or her temper, brings the feelings or rage under control. This act of control is *sàkòt jai*. In other words, *sàkòt jai* is the anger cut-off valve in the Thai language. Just as the anger reaches boiling point, the heat is turned off and the temper cools down and calmness (or at least resignation) is restored.

Cool Heart

jai yen   ใจเย็น

This is the Thai equivalent of a stiff upper lip in the face of adversity or provocation. A person may have suffered an emotional setback or disruption but he or she is able to feel (or give the appearance of feeling) collected and cool emotionally in the face of the problem. For example, Lek is stuck in a traffic jams for hours or has a flat tire on the expressway while driving at 100 kilometers per hour. The key is the ability to remain in control. Lek does not panic when the car tire blows out. Being stuck at Asoke and Sukhumvit intersection for forty minutes does not cause Lek to explode. If Lek does not show anger or cry, or express any other outward emotion, but deals with these incidents of distress with patience and composure, then it can be said that she is *jai yen*. A second meaning (perhaps less used) refers to the nature of a person who is slow and easy-going, and perhaps slightly lazy. In the first instance a person who can pull back from provocation without a negative reaction is an asset as an employee, friend, or family member. However, a person with a *jai yen* nature, within the second meaning, may prove unsuitable as your accountant.

Cut Heart

tàt jai   ตัดใจ

This is another way of saying "stop heart" or *yáp yáng châng jai.* A person is able to cut the impulse or the desire out of their heart. There is an object of desire that may be propelling him or her to go forward without thinking, as if they are on automatic pilot. A person with "cut heart" attempts to eliminate such non-reflective, reflex actions, and regain control and exercise self-restraint. Without *tàt jai* or *yáp yáng châng jai* a person's raw impulses and desires possess them.

Forgo Heart

òt jai   อดใจ

"Forgo heart" is another expression of restraint. The emphasis is on the ability to restrain one's immediate emotional response in an attempt to act more rationally. The translation into English as "forgo heart" suggests the heart is propelling us toward an emotional response which one ought to suppress. Thus if someone insults another with the heart phrase *khon jai yák* (a cruel and brutal person), one would seek to display *òt jai* and not respond with anger.

Recover Heart

jai maa pen kOOng   ใจมาเป็นกอง

"Recover heart" is used to mean that one has recovered from a moment of terror or loss. The "recovering hearted" person may have turned into the wrong street, and felt lost, stranded, only to discover, by pure chance, that his or her best friend has arrived in a car. The sight of sudden arrival of friend allows to him or her recover the feeling of terror which comes from being lost, isolated, stranded. One feels heartened and their courage and resolve suddenly return.

Restrain Heart

hàk jai   หักใจ

hàk òk hàk jai   หักอกหักใจ

hàk hâam jai   หักห้ามใจ

Someone daydreams about buying the multi-million-baht penthouse and toys with the idea of betting their life savings on a horse race in order to come up with the purchase price. But at the end of the day, the person controls their impulse and avoids the racetrack. The act of controlling their desire is *hàk jai*. Such a person is placing restrictions on themselves. The person with "restrain heart" is able to set the limits on the things they wish to do or acquire.

When their lover dies in a car crash or in war, then they must *hàk jai* to avoid the painful sense of loss which naturally arises. In a less dramatic circumstances: a person may *hàk jai* to avoid the feeling that comes with the end of a relationship or with the knowledge that it must end. Or when a wife discovers that her husband has a minor wife she must (under traditional social custom) restrain her heart. This tradition is not always kept in such circumstances.

Sleeping Heart

nOOn jai   นอนใจ

The person who feels *nOOn jai* is disconnected or uninterested in an event or action of another person which to most people would evoke some emotional response. The "sleeping heart" is a good definition for a passive person. Instead of taking action, such a person simply does nothing. This heart phrase is the Thai equivalent for the couch potato.

Soothing Heart

klÒOm jai   กล่อมใจ

The heart phrase refers to a person who, at the right moment, has the ability to act as an emotional caretaker for another who is depressed, troubled or worried. For example, one's best friend has received some bad news. In such circumstances, one wishes to *klÒOm jai* or soothe the friend through his or her emotional trauma. The "soothing heart" understands how to provide comfort and compassion to those who need such qualities at a time of crisis.

Stop Heart

yáp yáng châng jai   ยับยั้งชั่งใจ

"Stop heart" is a classic heart phrase for feelings of self-control. A person with such a heart is able to control their impulses and desires. If one is overweight, they want go on a diet immediately. If they drink or smoke too much, they want to quit drinking or smoking. Their desire to take control of their life in these cases is the feeling of *yáp yáng châng jai*.

The Light of the Heart which is the Center of the Dark World

jai sawàang klaang lôok mûuet   ใจสว่างกลางโลกมืด

The heart phrase has two meanings. The first is for the blind. Those who are born or later became blind; thus they live in the world with a disadvantage, but when others give them friendship, love and compassion the blind will have feelings of light entering the world of their heart and eliminating the darkness. The actions of others may bring a warm light into their otherwise dark world. The second meaning is connectecd with Buddhism and concentration practice. If one meditates on a regular basis, then he or she may experience feelings beyond emotion, a state of non-being which releases him or her from the darkness, pressures and demands of the world.

Heart Talk
Perception

Chapter 10

In Thai, certain perceptions such as understanding, satisfaction, and sincerity issue directly from the heart. The fact that trust is associated with the heart is a notion implicit in English. But, in English, we would rarely associate our understanding of what has been said or what another person has said to us with our heart—unless the conversation contained such an emotional component.

Understanding in this context, however, does not necessarily mean understanding in the sense of romantic or other feelings. These heart phrases suggest the limitation of English to provide accurate translations of the Thai heart phrase.

As indicated in the introduction, mind and heart have been for centuries divided in a fashion that is not true for the Thai language. In English, the mind would "understand" the rational, logic and analytical information, process that information and use it. While the heart might also "understand", it would be implicit in English that this understanding is qualitatively different in nature.

In Thai, the heart is involved in all matters of understandings. Finally, as this chapter illustrates, there is more than one Heart Talk phrase to express your sense of satisfaction—and, in each instance, the satisfaction is connected with your heart.

Another aspect of perception is imagination. This chapter ends with a review of several heart phrases that places the source of imagination square within the confines of the heart.

The descriptive language of the heart phrases include such ideas as: "read", "enter", "raised", "know", "premonition", and "thought".

Beauty
Beautiful to the Eye, Beautiful to the Heart
jarooen taa jarooen jai   เจริญตาเจริญใจ

The heart phrase is used to describe an aesthetically pleasing experience. The beauty experienced through the eye may be from a painting, a sunset, the latest designer dress, or the way a small child looks lovingly at her mother. Noticing a beautiful woman across the room will cause the viewer to feel *jarooen taa jarooen jai*. The aesthetic experience of witnessing a thing of beauty, whether a butterfly or a full moon, brings this condition of the heart into full bloom.

Pleasing to the Eye, Pleasing to the Heart

tÔOng jai   ต้องใจ

tÔOng taa tÔOng jai   ต้องตาต้องใจ

Red roses and chocolate cake are two items that are *tÔOng jai* or *tÔOng taa tÔOng jai* for many people. This can also be translated as "fondness heart" and used as a verb. What causes the heart to feel fondness for an object arises as the eye catches a pleasing object of desire. The initial excitement of finding this beautiful object is the essence of the phrase. One may be shopping and come across the perfectly pleasing dress, shirt, or necktie. In this case, what pleases the eye also pleases the heart.

Concentration

There are times when one wants to concentrate all of their efforts and energy to accomplish a task or reach a specific goal. Or one may concentrate their heart on another person, and by so doing, show a genuine interest in that person.

Concentrated Heart

jai jòt jai jÒO   ใจจดใจจ่อ

The heart phrase means one has developed the ability to fully focus on a project and to complete it without being sidelined by the usual distractions of life. A professional painter, writer, film director, athlete are examples of workers who require a "concentrated heart" in order to survive in fierce compention. At the same time, a "concentrated heart" may be the quality of being available to the emotional needs of someone. For instance, another person may be telling a long, emotional story and the listener pays full attention and gives understanding words and gestures as the story unfolds. The person telling the story will feel that such a listener is *jai jòt jai jÒO*.

Paying Attention Heart

phûu tâng jai fang   ผู้ตั้งใจฟัง

kaan tâng jai fang   การตั้งใจฟัง

A large part of concentration is paying attention to what someone else has to say. These heart phrases apply to certain formal relationships where paying attention is expected. For example, one listens and "pays attention heart" to the words of a doctor, a professor or a respected monk. Part of the paying attention is respect for their position, and part is for the benefit of the wisdom or advice such a person is giving. It is unlikely that one would hear or use either of these heart phrases in an informal setting such as with friends or colleagues.

Scattered Brain Heart

jai mây yùu kàp núuea kàp tua   ใจไม่อยู่กับเนื้อกับตัว

This heart phrases describes the absence of concentration. It describes someone who is doing one thing but thinking about something else. Thinking about the stock market and sticking a pen (rather than a key) into the lock on the front door. Attending a football match and is thinking about an MTV video. Noi leaves her ATM card in an ATM machine because she is thinking about how she is going to spend the money rather than concentrating on the business at hand. She loses her card as a result. The above are all examples of someone with a "scattered brain heart".

Stirred-up Heart

kuan jai   กวนใจ

The heart phrase means another person or thing is distracting one from a task they wish to perform. Such distraction reduces if not eliminates the ability to concentrate. One may wish to concentrate on reading the newspaper or on what is being said by one's spouse but the neighbor is mowing the lawn and the noise from the lawn mower interferes with their concentration. As a result, one cannot fully grasp the meaning of what is being read or said, and they may feel confused and mixed up about the message.

Forgetting

Cut from Memory of the Heart
lóp man pay jàak jai   ลบมันไปจากใจ

This heart phrase is the equivalent of the English expression, "Forget it." Usually the memory to be forgotten is associated with a painful or unpleasant experience. For instance, Lek believes that her boyfriend Vinai has a regular job and is well-regarded by the community. She discovers that, in fact, he is a car thief and is on the run from the police. After she breaks up with him, when her foreign friend asks about Vinai, Lek replies in a combination of Thai and English, "I have already *lóp Vinai pay jàak jai.*" I have already forgotten Vinai. As this example indicates, a person's name, an event or an object can be used in place of the Thai word *man* to express the notion that him, her or it has been deleted from the heart.

Imagination

The idea of imagination—which is linked with creativity—has several heart phrases. In the Thai language, a person's imagination is drawn from the heart.

Imagination Heart
kaan wâat phâap nay jai   การวาดภาพในใจ

Noi has been nominated for Best Actress of the Year at the annual Thai Oscars ceremony. On the day of the event, she is in her apartment dreaming of her moment of glory when her name is pulled out of the envelop and she is declared the winner. She imagines herself going on stage to receive the Oscar from M.C. Chatri, Thailand's most famous film director, and thinks of her acceptance speech. The essence of this heart phrase is imagining a future or past event. Imagination is not always glamorous and pleasant. One might imagine as they drive having a car crash. Another person might imagine what it would have been like to have been born in another country and within another family. Imagination is this mental ability to wonder "what if" about the present, future and past.

165
๑๖๕

Reflection Heart

phâap khûen nay jìt jai ภาพขึ้นในจิตใจ

This heart phrase is normally confined to the written (as opposed to spoken) word. Someone describes their trip to Los Angeles in such vivid terms that the listener is able to mentally picture Disneyland and Paramount Studio. The essence of "reflection heart" is the internal visualization of an experience, event, or place.

Intuition

Intuitive Heart

lá wáy nay thǎan thîi khâw jai ละไว้ในฐานที่เข้าใจ

A person feels that another person understands him or her without having to express fully their wishes or desires. For instance, the husband who senses his wife is tired during a long drive, suggests that they stop and have a cup of coffee. The essence of the heart phrase is the reliance upon intuition as a firm and reliable guide to understanding another's needs and acting upon that understanding. Being around someone with an "intuitive heart" ensures that non-verbal methods of communication will succeed in getting across the essential information concerning moods, wishes, dreams and desires. This kind of person simply knows what is appropriate for the situation.

Premonition Heart

sǎng hǑǑn jai สังหรณ์ใจ

When a person has a sixth sense or an intuitive feeling about someone or something then they have *sǎng hǑǑn jai*. They go into a business meeting with a premonition the deal will fall through, or they are driving home and have a feeling their spouse is in a bad mood or their *soi* has flooded with the afternoon rains. It matters less whether these things happened or not, it is the feeling about what will or will not happen in the future that gives you *sǎng hǑǑn jai*. This is a good quality in a private eye or other investigator.

Knowledge

Full Knowledge Heart

rúu yùu tem jai รู้อยู่เต็มใจ

The essence of this heart phrase is to have full knowledge of something but to act contrary to such knowledge. The person who knows that a small child cannot swim but allows her or him to go along to the swimming pool without a life guard present. The child nearly drowns. The knowledge at the point of making the decision to permit the child to swim alone is *rúu yùu tem jai*. The company executive who knows that Thursday is a national holiday in Thailand and that a foreign customer is coming to Bangkok with the express desire to meet and discuss financing with a banker but he or she says nothing to warn of the bank closing for the holiday. When the customer arrives and finds that no business can be transacted, that the trip was wasted, the customer becomes angry. The company executive is *rúu yùu tem jai* about the holiday, the closure of the bank and the customer's expectations in Bangkok.

Know Your Own Heart

rúu yùu kâE jai   รู้อยู่แก่ใจ

When someone has done a good deed, they know in their heart that they have added some goodness to the world. They comprehend the consequences of their words and actions on others. Thus if they do something bad or wrong which causes another to suffer harm then they also feel *rúu yùu kâE jai*. This is their conscience talking through their heart, monitoring the quality and kind of behavior one does or doesn't exhibit.

Raised Heart

khûen jai   ขึ้นใจ

When one learns a certain kind of information about the world by heart, then they become *khûen jai*. For instance, a person who has learned a poem, a Thai phrase, or another's face has rasied their heart. The acquistion of new information and the retention of this knowledge makes the person *khûen jai*.

Mistakes

Mistaken Heart

thalǎm jai   ถลำใจ

When someone realizes that they have made a mistake in loving or trusting another their heart is *thalǎm jai*. This is a more than average pain or regret heart condition. One feels cheated, let down, betrayed. Those are strong emotions. The company driver is discovered having cheated on his expense account. The empoyer had placed faith and trust in the honesty of the driver. His discovery of the theft is *thaläm jai*. His or her heart is mistaken about the driver, making him or her feel regret that he or she trusted him. In the political scene, factions of parties often form alliances and the leaders are seen shaking hands and smiling before the cameras and they proclaim that they are brothers forever and trust each other. Later, the alliance splits apart, even though the leaders promised this would never happen. One of the politicians may claim that the other's treachery comes as a shock and that he is sad about having trusted the other leader. The mistake of trusting the other is to *thaläm jai*.

Realization
Sudden Realization Heart

chùk jai	ฉุกใจ
sà dùt jai	สะดุดใจ

One has the abrupt realization that they have forgotten something. The memory of the forgotten thing returns in a flash. Another use is the sudden realization of something not understood before. For example, hearing for the first time the difference in the tone between the Thai words for tiger, shirt, doctor and horse. Leaving the house to go shopping, a person remembers an hour later that they have forgotten their credit card and cash. Another person misplaces their passport and suddenly wakes up in the middle of night and remembers where it has been misfiled. One has forgotten the name of one's third grade teacher, it is one of those experiences where the name is on the tip of the tongue, and suddenly for no reason the name pops out.

Satisfaction

As a person enters that state of feeling satisfied, they have a number of heart phrases to express their sense of satisfaction. Each phrase is a variation on the theme that one has done or accomplished something which has been the cause of the satisfaction. Akin to satisfaction are the feelings of relief and gratification, and there are heart phrases to express such feelings too.

Absolutely Agree Heart

tòk long plong jai	ตกลงปลงใจ

When one decides to trust another absolutely or makes a total commitment to them. In these circumstances, the person with an "absolutely agree heart" retains no reservations about the trustworthiness of the other. In their heart, they have no doubts about him or her.

Being in a State of a Full Heart
pen thîi phOO jai   เป็นที่พอใจ

An employee may *pen thîi phOO jai* with his or her boss. This translates into a state of full satisfaction concerning his or her working relationship with the employer. The same phrase can also be used in the context of various relationships: Between friends, relatives, co-workers, or spouses.

Conduct Shows an Unsatisfied Heart
sadà Eng kiri yaa mây phOO jai   แสดงกิริยาไม่พอใจ

This is a heart phrase used when another has made one feel disappointed, let down, or unhappy through their behavior. To the observer, a person's conduct demonstrates an act of misconduct. A person's lover shows up at three in the morning drunk and disheveled. Someone's son comes home with a report card filled with F marks. One's best friend runs off with his wife. If these things happened, chances are a person's heart will experience dissatisfaction with the conduct of another.

Fast Heart
than jai   ทันใจ

The heart phrase, "fast heart", means someone has responded or reacted quickly to a request. It is this absence of delay or excuses and the performance of exceptional service that is cause for using this phrase. For example, someone phones their travel agent and request a last minute booking on a flight to Hong Kong. The agent phones them back within ten minutes and confirms that they are booked and their ticket is ready for collection. The speed and efficiency of such service makes one feel *than jai* toward the travel agent.

Give enough to the Heart
tham hây phOO jai   ทำให้พอใจ

In this case, one is the agent who is giving the feeling of satisfaction to another person. A child is in a bad mood and begins to cry because the mother won't buy her sweets. The mother relents and buys the sweets and gives them to the daughter. The mother has in other words *tham hây phOO jai* her child. The same applies to the grown-up world when someone wants something and the absence of this object makes them unhappy; and she or he looks to another to provide this missing object.

Gratify Heart

thǔeng jai   ถึงใจ

This heart phrase is appropriate to express one's sense of accomplishment. A goal has been achieved and the person having crossed the finish line feels satisfaction. It may come from having completed a project at work, found the last word in a crossword puzzle, or having come to the end of a good book and found everyone lives in bliss forever. This heart phrase is also considered to be a slang expression.

Relieved Heart

baw jai   เบาใจ

Somone has passed their driving test and when told by the examining official of the success, the applicant is likely to feel a sense of relief. This is *baw jai*. An employee finishes his or her report by the required deadline. Another person has finished a good morning work out at the health club, or a round of golf at two under par. All these provide a sense of *baw jai*.

Satiated Heart

sǎa jai   สาใจ

sǎa kâE jai   สาแก่ใจ

nǎm jai   หนำใจ

This recent slang expression has entered the vocabulary and translates into a feeling of being pleased with one's self. What is pleasing to a person may not necessary be a good result for another. For example, someone who exacts revenge by taking another life may feel *säa jai*. On a more joyful note, members of an audience at a concert may experience a communal joyfulness (or "satisfied heart") while listening to the music. In this case, the person feeling *säa jai* has been the active agent in bringing about this feeling of satisfaction. *säa jai* has another meaning connected with "justice" (see Chapter 6).

Satisfied heart

jai rák   ใจรัก

When someone is thoroughly at one with what they are doing--the Zen state of perfect completion and satisfaction then they are *jai rák*. This is a good feeling of being in the groove of life, in a particular activity such as painting, collecting antiques, or taking Thai language lessons. Although, *jai rák* might be translated as "love heart", this would cause a misleading impression that the phrase is linked to romance and relationships when in fact it is used as an expression of keen interest in an activity.

Satisfied Heart

phOO jai   พอใจ

Perhaps the best known and most commonly used heart phrase for "satisfied heart" is this one. When a person is satisfied in their job, or relationship, they will have a "satisfied heart". If their spouse says he or she is *phOO jai*. That's a very good thing. It means that he or she is satisfied. But if he or she claims to be *mây phOO jai,* then he or she is saying that they are dissatisfied with an act, the failure to act, or with life itself. If one feels that their spouse is never content with what they do, then they may say their spouse is *mây khoey phOO jai.*

Satisfactory Heart

phueng jai   พึงใจ

phueng phOO jai   พึงพอใจ

This is a way to express one's feelings of satisfaction. Here is an example of a precise shading of meaning to capture the nature of satisfaction. Like many heart phrases, there are degrees of this feeling, and with each increase of feeling on the emotional scale, there is often another expression to measure the increase of emotional voltage. In this case, *phueng jai* is probably a greater feeling of satisfaction than *phOO jai.*

Sincerity

The exploration of feelings in a relationship often are about the degree of sincerity of the people involved. Each person wants to feel another person is sincere in his or her words and actions. That there is no deception or hidden agenda involved. Conversely, a person wishes others close to them will believe and trust them. These heart phrases provide a rich variety of expressions related to trust (or distrust); and provide a way to ask about the sincerity of another.

Believe Heart

chûea jai	เชื่อใจ
wáy núea chûea jai	ไว้เนื้อเชื่อใจ

The heart phrase is similar to *wáy jai*. One trusts another person, and this expresses itself by the belief in the sincerity of the other person's heart. Or one asks another to *chûea jai* them; to believe in what they have told them. One is an hour late for an appointment and they want the person waiting to believe they were caught in heavy traffic. In Bangkok, this reason is normally taken at face value. But if one shows up four hours late with lipstick on their collar and asks their lover to believe they were late because of traffic, it is likely she won't *chûea jai* her partner.

Showing Truth Heart

sadà Eng khwaam jing jai   แสดงความจริงใจ

One does not only feel sympathy with another's suffering or failure, they demonstrate their feelings of care and support to the victim of life's misfortunes. This feeling inside a person's heart is *sadà Eng khwaam jing jai*. The sense is similar to *hěn jai* or *nám jai*. Another example of heart words wrapped around the feeling which are sensitive to other people's emotional traumas.

Showing Water Heart

sadà Eng nám jai   แสดงน้ำใจ

A person shows or demonstrates their sympathy with another. This is another variation of showing the truth residing in a person's heart. Often this may be a small gesture. Dropping a few coins in a beggar's bowl. Giving up one's seat on the bus for an elderly passenger.

Trust Heart

waang jai   วางใจ

Trust heart" is another variation of *wáy jai*. Also *wáy waang jai*. Thus demonstrating that the trusting heart is a valued quality amongst the Thais, and the appreciation for such a heart is honored by a number of different ways of paying tribute to a such a person.

Truth Heart

khwaam jing jai   ความจริงใจ

If one desires for others to believe that they are sincere, they are asking them to believe that they possess *khwaam jing jai*. One's lover, spouse, friends and children wish to believe he or she is sincere in his or her words and action. This is a common heart phrase, which indicates the importance that Thais place on sincerity.

Temptation

Temptation Heart

lÔO taa lÔO jai   ล่อตาล่อใจ

The eye sees what the heart desires but cannot have. The person who loves lobster but has an allergic reaction if she or he eats it will be tempted to eat a particularly delicious looking lobster but will stop herself or himself from doing so. A person passes through a shopping mall and sees the latest computer game and wants to buy it. Unfortunately he or she does not have the money and must continue on walking, empty handed.

Understanding

When one wishes to communicate ideas about learning, comprehension, or failure to comprehend, these heart phrases are useful.

Clearly Understood Heart

sÓOm khwaam khâw jai   ซ้อมความเข้าใจ

This heart expression is employed to make certain that someone has clearly understood what one has sought to communicate. In other words, as a way to double check that a message has been conveyed and understood, *sÓOm khwaam khâw jai* is a useful phrase.

Enter Heart

khâw jai   เข้าใจ

A frequently heard phrase is *khâw jai* which translates as understanding what someone else has said or meant by what they have said. It may be in the form of a question to determine if one has understood what has been said. And if a person has understood, the correct reply to such a question is to repeat the phrase *khâw jai*. This literally means what the other person has said has "entered your heart". This is not limited to understanding the expression of emotions but any source of information that has been communicated. From understanding a technical manual on operating a computer to whether a person has properly filled out a bank form. This a state of understanding of what has been said, demonstrated, or written.

Essence Heart

jai khwaam   ใจความ

This is a linguistic heart phrase used to explore the meaning, substance, or the gist of a heart word or phrase. For instance, the gist of *säng hÖOn jai* or "premonition heart" is the intuitive feeling that someone has about an event or person or thing. When in doubt about the meaning of a heart phrase ask a native Thai speaker the *jai khwaam* of the phrase in question. Often the *jai khwaam* provided will not only increase one's knowledge of the heart phrase but will speak volumes about the speaker's own personality, background and interests.

Know Heart

rúu jai   รู้ใจ

When a person finds that Zen state of total intimacy they may want to utter the expression: *rúu jai*. You know another person's heart. This is not a heart phrase to be said lightly as idle pillow talk. For a Thai speaker, it is one thing to "Measure Heart" or *wát jai*. But to truly know another's heart is a quantum leap in knowledge. In your life you may know only a few hearts: your own (if you are lucky), that of your father and mother (if you have had a Thai upbringing the chances are great this will be true) and from there the list falls off radically for many Thai speakers.

Misunderstanding the Heart

khâw jai phìt เข้าใจผิด

If one has misunderstood what has been communicated and acted upon that misunderstanding then, when asked why the person acted or behaved in that fashion, once the mistake comes to light, it is appropriate to say *khâw jai phìt*. The literal translation would be the information has gone into the heart the wrong way. Either one can not make sense of it, or one acted on the misunderstanding. For example, if one makes an appointment for a meeting at ten in the morning and the other person believes the appointment was intended for ten at night, they would have misunderstood the time of the meeting, arriving twelve hours late. Upon talking with the other person after the error has been discovered about the meeting time, an appropriate response to the mix up would be *khâw jai phìt*.

Read Heart

àan jai อ่านใจ

When another person has suffered an emotional set back, one seeks the true cause of the upset. If it is a close friend or a family member, the "read heart" person may know without being told the cause of the suffering or misery. With a stranger is it more difficult to read their heart because they are not part of their lives. Nonetheless, if one sees a mother crying beside the body of her child, even though she is a stranger, most people will be able to read the grief in her heart.

Remember Raised Heart

jam khûen jai จำขึ้นใจ

jam khûen jai means to learn by heart. One remembers a friend's birthday, lunch appointments, telephone number, or street address and by so doing they feel *jam khûen jai*.

Silent Reading Heart

àan nay jai อ่านในใจ

This heart phrase concerns the processing of reading. When one is reading a book or report, concentrating on its contents and wishing to take the substance of the printed word directly into their heart. "Silent reading heart" is often used in the context of study and examination. It is mostly employed by students attending schools and universities, or lip readers as they mouth every word in a restaurant menu.

Think Inside Heart

núek yùu nay jai   นึกอยู่ในใจ

When one thinks to themself then they experience *núek yùu nay jai*. Some people have on-going internal dialogs with themselves. Should I take the train to Chiang Mai on Saturday? I would like a salary increase, now if only I could find a way to ask.... That is a beautiful, attractive person sitting at the next table, should I go over and start a conversation? These are examples of what goes on inside when one "thinks inside heart" or *núek yùu nay jai*.

Understanding Heart

jai khǎw jai raw   ใจเขาใจเรา

This heart phrase is an expression of empathy with others: an attempt to understand another person as one understands oneself. "Understanding heart" is a popular expression taught to Thai children and is not difficult for them to comprehend. The emotional terrain is similar to the that occupied by *hěn jai* or *nám jai*. In the context of friendship, it is a call for sympathy and understanding. The phrase can also be linked to the working of the *kreeng jai* system. In this context, "understanding heart" rests on empathy for those who occupy a social rank either above or below the person seeking the empathy.

This heart phrase is the equivalent of the "Golden Rule of Hearts". If one wishes to be treated equally and fairly then they must give such treatment to others. Thus the boss who has a rule that his staff must work until 8.00 p.m. but he or she leaves the office at 5.00 p.m. would be in violation of this golden rule of hearts because his rule applying to others does not apply to himself or herself.

Understanding Another's Heart

nâng nay hǔa jai   นั่งในหัวใจ

The heart phrase comes from a Thai proverb: "To sit in another heart is to have knowledge of their mind and soul." Thus it is putting oneself in the place of another in order to know how they think and feel. With such understanding it becomes easier to anticipate the other person's wants, desires and moods. The essence of this heart phrase is the intimate (insider's) knowledge of another's mental landscape and how to follow the paths to happiness and to avoid the drop off into despair and disappointment.

Heart Talk
Choice

Chapter 11

Each day in a hundred different contexts one is confronted with a number of choices to make. Indeed the average day is about choosing among options. A person makes judgments and decisions about what to wear, where to eat dinner, who to telephone, and where to plan a holiday. It is not uncommon for someone not to be able to make up their mind. They are uncertain what to do, where to go, what to choose. In the Thai language the heart plays a large role in the expressions concerning the ability to make judgments and decisions.

In this chapter, heart phrases illustrate a range of statements about the process of making or changing a decision or plan. One has the chance to explore certain patterns involved in the following, changing, weighing, and wavering of the heart. In each heart phrase, a nuance is revealed about the way a person has made, changed, or failed to make a decision or judgment.

One has the chance to express themselves about free will as well. It is an important value in Thai culture that a person is "free" to make their own choices, and there are a number of heart phrases which reflect this deep-seated cultural value.

Decision Making
Aspired Heart

măay jai   หมายใจ

One sees a beautiful girl waiting at the bus stop and the observer feels like striking up a conversation. He experiences a feeling of attraction and this naturally leads him to try and establish contact. "Aspired heart" is the desire a person feels in such circumstances.

Endure Heart

khà ng jai   แข็งใจ

A person falls down on the street and injured their ankle, and after picking themself up, he or she limps that last mile home. Along the way they have to *khà ng jai*. The notion of "endure heart" is that a person is forcing themself forward despite the pain they are suffering. When someone has a task that they would rather not perform but are compelled through circumstances or position to carry it out, then they too must *khà ng jai*.

Fall into Heart

kaan tòk long jai   การตกลงใจ

This use of "fall into heart" is the noun form of having made a decision. Thus the decision to take a new job or ask one's lover to marry him or her is *kaan tòk long jai*. The decision concerns an important opportunity for the person who is deciding on a course of action to actually do something.

Fall into the Heart

tòk long jai   ตกลงใจ

A person decides to see a film, or eat at a new restaurant or have their hair styled in a new fashion. To decide on any course of action is *tòk long jai*. This is a verb form. This is a common and important phrase in Thai. When the time comes to make a decision, and a person decides what to do, what they want, or what they value, then they have "fallen into the heart".

Get Ready Heart

tham jai   ทำใจ

The essence is preparation. There are many circumstances in life when one is called upon to confront an unpleasant task or duty. For instance, visiting a terminally ill person in hospital who is hooked up to a life support system. Before such a visitation, the person must *tham jai* before entering the patient's room. The student who has failed his or her examination must *tham jai* before handing over the report card to his or her father. The employee who has lost a customer for her or his company due to a careless mistake and must explain this mistake to the boss must *tham jai* before such a meeting.

Heart Fast

jai rew ใจเร็ว

The verbal spin of "heart fast" translates as someone who feels he or she has acted with undue haste. When such a person makes a quick decision in response to another person or an event, and afterwards he or she comes to the realization that the decision was flawed or wrong. Such decisions are often the product of time pressures arising at that moment. A person may feel that they are *jai rew* at that moment they realize their haste.

Intent Heart

jong jai จงใจ

If one intends while at work during the morning to phone his or her friend, spouse, colleague, or lover later that evening, then he or she *jong jai*. They have formed an intention to do some specific act. The person with "intent heart" may intend to go out during your lunch hour and buy a gift for a friend's birthday. The feeling that comes from forming one's intention is *jong jai*. It is not the actual carrying out of the intention but the emotion that arises having made a decision to do something later.

Preparing Heart

tream jai เตรียมใจ

The essence is the feeling of dread or fear of confronting a certain situation or state of affairs. A patient on the eve of a serious operation will "prepare their heart" for the operation and this may bring on feelings of fear. A worker who repeatedly makes careless mistakes in her or his work is told they have an appointment to meet the boss to discuss their sloppy work is likely to be fearful in preparing themselves for the appointment. The person who is fearful of flying will prepare themselves for the flight they must board to travel abroad *tream jai* before such a meeting.

Resist Heart

jai sûu ใจสู้

One feels like they want to do something over again. The report they wrote wasn't quite good enough because some information was left out. Or they played a bad round of golf and wanted to return to the course after lunch for another round to practise their game. This sense that somehow one failed and wishes to return for another chance to do something better or to do it right is *jai sûu*. Perhaps Noi had a quarrel with her lover and failed to explain her position as fully as she had wished, and she looks for the chance to explain her position once again.

Spontaneous Heart

than jai   ทันใจ

He or she wants to do something immediately, like take off for the weekend to Chiang Mai or Koh Samet. The "spontaneous heart" lives on a moment's notice. They phone a friend and invite him or her over to their apartment to use the swimming pool. The friend accepts and arrives half an hour later. The person extending the invitation feels that person who has arrived on such short notice is *than jai*.

Sure Heart

nÊE jai   แน่ใจ

One may wish to make an absolute judgment or decision, or they may wish another person to make such a judgment or decision. For example, someone discusses taking a possible trip to Chiang Mai with Lek. He may want to ask her if she is *nÊE jai* about traveling on the proposed dates. In this context, *nÊE jai* is a way of expressing commitment to a decision, or the degree of certainty being made about a judgment. He has offered to buy Lek a gold chain, and she asks him if he is certain. To say one is *nÊE jai* gives that reassurance that they are sure in their heart and about their desire to follow through on their judgment or decision.

Weight Heart

châng jai   ชั่งใจ

In order to reach a decision, he or she carefully weighs the pros and cons, considering all the possibilities of whether to go or stay at home, to walk or drive to the office, to sit or stand at a reception. Each decision requires a person to assess the relative benefits of alternative courses of action. The "weight heart" process is the way of reaching an ultimate decision among competing possibilities. Deciding which path has more merit, more benefit or more reward is *châng jai*.

Free Will

The idea of free will relies upon several important metaphors such as to follow and master one's heart to express subjection to the control of others and the exercise of personal freedom. These Thai phrases recognize the balance between independence and interdependence, between the individual and the family, and the constant play between getting one's way and giving way to the wishes of another. Associated with free will is the notion of willpower for which there is also a heart phrase.

As One's Heart

dàng jai   ดั่งใจ

yàang jai   อย่างใจ

dang jai   ดังใจ

One has freedom of choice to do something or the ability to do what they wish. The essence of these heart phrases is the free will to act independently. There is an absence of external pressure or intervention which forces a certain decision. The decision-maker comes to the decision without coercion or influence. This is an ideal state for making a decision though one rarely found in reality. No one is telling another what they must or have to do. This is the perfect state, whether in a job, relationship, or in life, that one has the good fortune to act according to their personal desires. As long as a person's wishes determine what they will or will not do, then they will continue to exist in this emotional state. *tham mäy dâay yàang jai* means a person does not have the free will or free choice.

Follow One's Heart

taam jai   ตามใจ

This is an extremely important heart phrase. One can *taam jai* themselves, their child, spouse, friend, employee, maid, etc. In one way, it means spoiling the other; in other variations, it means giving the other person control to decide whether to do something. It can be used as an escape valve that prevents someone else losing face. It can provide the other person an "out". Whether the decision is about what TV show to watch or which restaurant to go to, it is common for a Thai speaker to defer the decision as to choice to another person, especially where that person is considered above them in the social ladder or older than they or their mother or father.

Lost Oneself Heart

phÉE jai tua eeng   แพ้ใจตัวเอง

To experience "lost oneself heart" is to have the sense of discouragement. For instance, a smoker feels such a lost heart, having kicked the habit only to pick it up again six months later. The heart phrase means one has been defeated by the strength of their own desires which they have not succeeded in mastering. A person who is on a strict diet and then gains back the weight only to repeat the cycle of diet and gain once again is also "lost yourself heart". Such person knows that they should stop a certain course of conduct but can't find the willpower to do so.

Master of Heart

pen jâw hǔa jai   เป็นเจ้าหัวใจ

This is the opposite of *tham dây yàang jai*. One is subject to the control or dictates of another so that they really have little control over their own destiny. This is a bad news heart message. The heart phrase means there is the absence of free will or choice. If someone complains about feeling *pen jâw hǔa jai*, it means someone close to them has been pushing their wants, demands, desires onto the other. Change their hair style, change their clothes, shoes or the way they walk and talk. The person with a "master of heart" is often a bully. Their actions smack of thought control and a heavy hand to control the actions of another person. If one finds themself constantly resorting to this heart phrase it is possible that they have found themself on the wrong side of a control freak and with this Thai phrase the person who is the object of a "master of hearts" is screaming to get out.

Uncertainty

There are several heart phrases to illustrate that deciding upon a course of action is difficult. By taking one path, another path is abandoned. By buying one dinner, another dinner is excluded. Sometimes there are too many choices; other times there are individuals who by force of personality find it difficult to make up their minds.

Change of Heart

plèan jai　เปลี่ยนใจ

Change of heart" is a common heart phrase. A person changes his or her mind about ordering rice and orders french fries, or changes his or her mind two or three times in one morning about what colors to wear—in other words, there are a wide range of possible changes involved—the verb *plèan jai* is the proper heart phrase. In Thai one does not change their mind; they change their heart.

Changeable Heart

phlǒe jai　เผลอใจ

This heart phrase is similar to "change heart" discussed above. A few examples, however, illustrate that this phrase has its own sphere of meaning. For instance, two people have been dating for two years. The boyfriend returns to England for a couple of months. His girlfriend, shortly after his departure, meets another man who is attractive and interesting and within a week, she has a new boyfriend. In this case the ex-girlfriend *phlǒe jai* with her ex-boyfriend.

A changeable heart is not always a bad attribute in a person. Say Lek is much taller than Vinai. Because there is a cultural expectation that men should be taller than their lover or spouse, Lek dismisses the idea of a relationship with Vinai. Vinai, as it turns out, is a very nice guy with a good heart and after awhile Lek no longer thinks that the height difference is that important. *phlǒe jai* might equally apply to changes in perception about weight, race, age, and social status: All of these factors initially may cause one person to exclude or discount another as a possible friend, colleague, lover or spouse.

Confused Heart

yûng yâak jai　ยุ่งยากใจ

In some cases, the choice between alternatives causes confusion. The person facing the choice falls into a state of emotional chaos. Or the "confused heart" may be a pretext for a failure to act when a person wishes to retain the best of all worlds. For example, the man with three minor wives is faced with a delegation who demands that he select one as the "major" wife. After considering this demand, the husband is confused as to which of the minor wives ought to be selected.

Hesitate Heart

sǑOng jìt sǑOng jai   สองจิตสองใจ

The "hesitate heart" is a Hamlet-like person and can't make up their mind whether they want to holiday at the beach or the mountains, take a wife or a lover, a house or an apartment, a sports car or a sedan. Such a person is forever going through the possibilities without ever making a firm decision. The chronically indecisive person is definitely a candidate for inclusion in *sǑOng jìt sǑOng jai* hall of fame.

Unstable Heart

jai ruan ree   ใจรวนเร

"Unstable heart" is another way of saying *sǑOng jìt sǑOng jai*— (hesitate heart). Like *lang lee jai*, the expression *jai ruan ree* shows that Thai has a number of phrases for the indecisive, those approaching the exist ramp but not knowing whether to take it or move straight ahead.

Waver Heart

lang lee jai   ลังเลใจ

If someone spends a long time deciding what course of action to take, or which alternative to follow, this kind of uncertain, indecisive, wavering behavior is *lang lee jai*. This is the first of several heart phrases to cover the Hamlets of the world who are forever asking "to be or not to be" in many circumstances of life.

Heart Talk
Romance

Chapter 12

This chapter contains Heart Talk Phrases which most lovers who are fluent in the Thai language wish to hear from the object of their affection. Every language has its "Pillow Talk", and the Thai language is no exception. "Pillow Talk" is found in the metaphors linked to the heart. When one uses one of these heart phrases, remember that the listener is expecting the speaker to reveal the true condition of his or her feelings. In most cases, the Thai listener has an experienced ear, judging each heart phrase with a view to determining if it is sincere.

The Thais are world class experts on knowing whether one's expression of heart and the actual status of the heart match. Whether the speaker is being genuine or is merely trying to please with a pleasant phrase. The quickest way to lose credibility is to use a heart phrase for an ulterior motive, that is in an effort to gain something from the listener rather than communicate a true emotional state of being.

A number of the heart phrases appearing in this chapter have appeared in earlier chapters. For the die-hard romantic a review of such heart phrases from the point of view of romance is a useful exercise.

A good place to start is with heart phrases about commitment and then to examine the heart phrases one might find inside a full cycle of romance: Boy wishes to meet girl and suffers until he finds her, then boyfriend and girlfriend have an argument and the relationship ends with the girl walking out, and the boy is left to nurse his emotional wounds. Of course the cycle is the same where the girl wishes to meet boy. At each point in the cycle there is a heart phrase.

Commitment

There are romantic relationships that last a day and others that last a life time. The degree of personal commitment to the relationship is conveyed in a number of heart phrases. The common link with each phrase is the importance a special person occupies in the life of another. Given this chapter is about romance—one kind of a relationship—the object of communication is assumed to be a spouse or lover.

Body and Heart

tháng kaay lÉ jai   ทั้งกายและใจ

The heart of romance is when two people achieve that state of being where they feel a communion of Body and Soul. The heart phrase *tháng kaay lÉ jai* is that threshold beyond *plong jai rák*. When one's spouse or lover whispers *tháng kaay lÉ jai* it is the ultimate Zen state of commitment when the bodies and souls of two people merge and there is now a sense of oneness. She has held nothing back and neither has he; they exist together as body and soul. One is deep in the heartland of romance before using *tháng kaay lÉ jai*. By doing so, the man becomes the woman's hero and she becomes his heroine, and they are in a romantic epic of their own making.

Confident Heart

mân jai   มั่นใจ

To have a "confident heart" means a person is confident of their feelings about their spouse or lover. In the context of romance, the confidence is specifically about the relationship and the other person's commitment to the relationship. To say one feels *mân jai* is regarded as an expression of commitment between two people in a relationship. When one person asks their lover about his or her feelings concerning the relationship, and the lover replies by using this expression, it means she or he trusts them and is committed to being with them.

Contract of One's Heart

săn yaa jai   สัญญาใจ

"Contract of one's heart" is another weighty emotional heart phrase. One has committed their heart to a permanent relationship or marriage. This commitment is *săn yaa jai*—it is one person's contract with their heart. And the terms are clear: he or she is in the relationship for keeps. This is not idle conversation for the first date. This is not dating talk at all. The language of contract means one has sealed a lover's bargain for staying the course over the long haul. Break this contract and the damages for the contract breaker to worry about are not ones their lawyer can protect them against.

Gold Chain Around One's Heart

sôo thOOng khlÓOng jai   โซ่ทองคล้องใจ

The "gold chain around one's heart" is a feeling Thai parents may have about their children in orbit around their lives. Also, it is an expression for the feeling children have about their parents. The heart phrase conveys a good feeling or a feeling of wellness. It is not limited to parent-child and may be used between lovers.

Like the heart phrase below, this one is the real "inside stuff" on what Thai speakers say to express that special relationship. It would be unusual for a non-native speaker to know and use this phrase. By so doing, it is likely to draw an amazed smile. The spin is this, "An emotional gravity holds us in a tight orbit, and nothin', but nothin' ain't gonna pull us apart."

Irrevocable Heart

plong jai rák   ปลงใจรัก

The irreversible feeling of love is *plong jai rák*. One has given in their heart to another in a way that makes it impossible for them to withdraw from the relationship. The notion of "irrevocably" is weighty and meaningful in any language. If wishes to use *plong jai rák* it should be understood that "irrevocable heart" is an expression of a lifelong commitment. To revoke the irrevocable is probably an exempted risk on Thai life insurance policy; one should check it before carelessly using this heart phrase. These are the words every Thai (indeed everyone) wishes to hear—but not as *phûut aw jai* or flattering talk.

Iris of the Heart

kÊEw taa duang jai   แก้วตาดวงใจ

The person who is the "iris of the heart" is the most important or vital person residing in the center of one's heart. This is the NASA command center. Every emotional thing a person puts into orbit comes from here. One wants to be programed into this place in their spouses or lover's heart. It is common for Thais to say the most important thing in a mother's heart is her children. And a daughter will invariably say her mother is the most important thing in her heart. It is less common for a lover to use this phrase; but when used in the romantic context what proceeds is often an emotional meltdown.

My Heart

jai duang níi   ใจดวงนี้

This romantic heart phrase means that one is committed to another. It is an expression of giving one's heart to that special person in their life. Each person would like for their lover or spouse to proclaim, "I love you and *jai duang níi* is for you only."

Cycle of Romance

Breathing Together Heart

mii jai hây kan   มีใจให้กัน

Early into the romantic cycle it is common for lovers to experience a closeness and oneness. It is as if they are breathing as one being. Thus the "breathing together heart" is the honeymoon phase of the relationship. The ultimate discovery of defects and flaws is for a later stage in the cycle. For the moment, the lovers are in peace and harmony with one another. They are fulfilled and satisfied. And more importantly, they are in love with one another.

The essence of the heart phrase is to the love two people feel towards each other. This phrase can be used to ask a question about whether another person loves them. A couple has been friends for a long time and this grows into love and one day, one them acknowledges this transition from friendship into love by using this phrase.

Capture Another's Heart

khàyûm hǔa jai   ขยุ้มหัวใจ

This is a slang heart phrase for describing the feeling that comes when another person has captured their heart. The meaning is they want a relationship with this person, the feeling of love and commitment are implicit in the phrase as well. Lek may confide to her friend Noi, that Charles with whom she has been having a relationship via the internet has captured her heart.

Cold Heart

nǎaw jai   หนาวใจ

"Cold heart" is the opening scene prior to the commencement of a love affair. A man or woman who claims to feel *nǎaw jai* is giving a signal that he or she wishes to have a relationship with another and is suffering from the lack of such a relationship. The heart phrase is the stuff of poetry, films, and novels. The emotional state is like an arctic cold front which blows through a person's heart and leaves them with the feeling of aloneness; in this snowbound world of the heart, their life in the world is cold, and they experience *nǎaw jai*. When this inner sense of loneliness occurs then the desire arises to seek refuge in a relationship. On the other hand, a man or a woman who is constantly complaining of this emotional state might be said to be *khîi nǎaw jai*. The expression refers to the nature of such a person which suggests a negative quality.

Depressed Heart

rá thom jai   ระทมใจ

The "depressed heart" is the final emotional state in the romantic cycle of lovers meeting, one lover leaving the other, and the left person feeling depressed. The term is used primarily in the context of a love affair that has ended or is heading toward its final destruction. The heart phrase is similar to *pòdet jai* but it conveys a greater sense of depression. When one's lover runs off with his or her best friend then he or her will feel *rá thom jai*.

Heaven in the Chest, Hell in the Heart

sawǎn nay òk narók nay jai   สวรรค์ในอกนรกในใจ

The literal translation is that one feels heaven in one's chest but hell inside one's heart. The lovers no longer are breathing as one person. Conflicts have emerged. The inevitable problems of adjustment have given way to a period of compromise where one or both lovers feel that they have the best and worst of worlds inside the relationship. The heart experiences an emotional schizophrenia. Whether the heaven part dominates or the hell part does will depend on a number of factors within the relationship. Or it may be that the balance between heaven and hell is roughly equal and the relationship struggles along without any firm resolution.

Hurt Heart

hŭa jai ráaw raan   หัวใจร้าวราน

"Hurt Heart" occurs along with the "heaven and hell heart" in the love affair cycle. After finding the person to rid one of the feeling of *näaw jai* the lover splits from the scene. Now he or she finds themself in the possession of another kind of broken heart; one without the feeling for revenge. This feeling for the lover should be distinguished from *jèp jai*, which is a broken heart, for which the person may seek revenge. When dealing with broken hearts, it is important to distinguish between emotional conditions where the hurt is turned inward, such as *hŭa jai ráaw*, which is the language of poetry, songs, films and novels where a love affair has ended.

Melting Heart

jai lá laay   ใจละลาย

The "melting heart" is another heart phrase for disappointment in love. The woman leaves the man and he feels disappointed in love. The emotional state is one of heavy, hurt feelings over the loss of a loved one.

Possess Another's Heart

khrOOng jai   ครองใจ

The emotional message is that by possessing another's heart there is an obligation to look after and take care of the emotional well being of that person. Lovers can employ this heart phrase when talking about their feelings. Often it is used among friends to describe how they feel about their loved ones. Sometimes the heart phrase pops up in commercial advertising as well. For instance, it has been used to sell house paint. The paint which is claimed to be of very good quality possesses the heart of the people who love their house.

Endearments

The use of terms of endearment has a different cultural basis in Thai than in English. English speakers in a relationship often employ "darling" and "sweetheart" to refer to a special loved one. However, such endearments are rarely used among Thai couples. To use one of the endearments described below would be done for effect, as a kind of joke but almost never as an expression of affection.

Many Thais would consider the use of such endearments in the class of cartoon language. Use of these terms are not thought of as sign of affection. One may wish to come across as Humphrey Bogart using a "sweetheart" line when what is being heard is a Jay Leno or David Letterman line. There are a number of endearments which if used will allow one to practice their stand-up comic act with their Thai lover or spouse.

Best Heart

sùt jai   สุดใจ

It is possible to find Thai women with the name *sùt jai. sùt jai* is, however, another heart phrase which doubles up one's Thai lover with laughter if used as a romantic term of endearment.

Medicine Heart

yaa jai   ยาใจ

yaa in earlier times was used as a verb meaning to patch a boat, and the same word in the noun form also means "medicine." This is another term of endearment like sweetheart or darling which a Thai might bestow as a name for their child. But if one tries to use it romantically as saying the other is medicine for their heart then they will be greeted with laughter. This is a good line if one wishes to create a Thai laugh track but otherwise to be avoided.

Sweet Heart

wǎan jai   หวานใจ

This is "sweetheart" in Thai. But should one employ the endearment, one's spouse or lover may say that they are a *pàak wǎan* or sweet mouthed. The chances are very high it would be met with a laugh and treated as a joke, and unless one is aware of this cultural difference the joke may be on them. The concept of *wǎan* is associated with a gentle, soft-natured, and innocent person. But this heart phrase is thought excessive and insincere.

Infatuation

Love's second cousin is infatuation. An emotion sometimes confused with love itself.

Infatuated Heart

khwǎn jai   ขวัญใจ

khwǎn jai is the appropriate expression that applies when a person becomes infatuated with another. The subject of the infatuation may be a movie star, such as Bird Thongchai is for a large number of Thai women. For Thai men, the Thai singer Mai Jaroenpura causes them to experience bouts of *khwǎn jai* as well. The "infatuated heart" is not limited to the teen years and extends to the office, the classroom, or a member's club.

Intimacy

Romance is marked by intimacy. The closeness, joy and happiness that springs from an intimate relationship is the subject of a number of heart phrases. This section provides a few examples of how to increase the heart vocabulary to express one's intimate feelings toward another.

Catch Heart

jàp jai   จับใจ

A person who uses *jàp jai* is able to express his emotional feelings of intimacy in a highly touching, persuasive fashion to another person. *jàp jai* means to have captured another's heart with expressions of feeling.

Joyful Heart

chûuen jai   ชื่นใจ

Intimacy and closeness also create an emotional state of being joyful. One person in the relationship gives the other a special amulet and she or he will likely feel *chûuen jai*. The definition of intimacy is understanding what brings joy to the heart of another and acting upon that knowledge. What does it take to make someone joyful? This is a list for all lovers to work on together.

Merged Heart

klOOy jai   กลอยใจ

To get one's spouse or lover's attention, one can use the "merged heart" phrase to convey to her or him that he or she is their *klOOy jai*. The heart phrase conveys the sense that two people are emotionally and spiritually merged into a single person. Most often, this expression is used in the context of a mother and child relationship. In a romantic relationship, however, it can be used with someone a person loves and cares for very much.

Open Heart

pòet jai   เปิดใจ

When two people are close enough as to disclose their most secret, hidden feelings to each other, then they are *pòet jai*. They have an "open heart" with one anohther. The heart phrase may also apply outside an intimate relationship, to an entertainer such as a singer, who has created a bond with his or her audience.

Soft Heart

jai ÒOn   ใจอ่อน

It is said that intimacy softens the heart, takes away the rough, harsh, judgmental edges. A person who has a soft heart does many things for his friends, family, children and is *jai ÒOn*. Such a person places his personal relationship higher than his self-interest. The person who has *jai ÒOn* is giving, respectful, and thoughtful in his or her relations. Unlike *jai dii*, which may apply to an isolated act of kindness, *jai ÒOn* is more the general pattern of behavior over a long period of time.

Touch One to the Quick

jîi hǔa jai   จี้หัวใจ

The heart phrase means to be touched emotionally by something or someone. Maybe a scene in a film makes a person feel sad. Perhaps getting flowers makes them feel happy. Either way a person may feel *jîi hǔa jai*. In the context of a romantic relationship, the small gestures of love such as a phone call, a card, a gift will likely to the heart of the person receiving it.

Love is implicit in many of the heart phrases contained under the headings of commitment and loyalty. There are a number of heart phrases included below which deal specifically with excessive feelings of love for another.

Addicted Heart

tìt jai	ติดใจ
tìt òk tìt jai	ติดอกติดใจ
tìt núea tÔOng jai	ติดเนื้อต้องใจ

This heart phrase has already been explored in Chapter 9 as an example of lack of control. In the context of a romantic relationship, one person may develop an addiction to another. The addiction can lead to obsessive conduct such as repeated phone calls. In the case of a break up, the "addictive heart" may follow the script from the classic movie *Fatal Attraction*.

Brimming Over Heart

lón jai	ล้นใจ

This heart phrase is used to provide emphasis of feeling. Thus a person who wishes to declare that his or her feelings of affection or love rise significantly above the ordinary may resort to this heart phrase. For example, Lek wishes to express her feelings of love to Vinai, and she says, "*rák khun jon lón jai*". I love you so much my heart brims over with love." Thus *lón jai* acts as an exclamation point added to an expression of love.

Love Sickness

khây jai	ไข้ใจ

"Love sickness" befalls the true romantic. They see someone across a crowded room and fall in love. Or at the office they are secretly in love with a colleague. What is at work in this "love sickness" is the tendency to love someone at a distance. The landscape of this love ballet is deep inside the person's own imagination and dreams. The love is locked inside their head. There is a second meaning for *khây jai*. A man has the kind of relationship where he and his lover are so wrapped up in love that even a short separation causes him to experience *khây jai*.

Pouring Out of the Heart

thee jai   เทใจ

This is the right romantic heart talk phrase where one person has poured out his or her feelings of love for the other. To express one's feelings of love is where this heart phrase is used. *thee jai* is descriptive of the act of expressing one's love for another. Thus when Mai proclaims her love will endure well "into the late afternoon of the next life" for Harry, she is pouring out her heart to him.

Really Pleased with Heart

sùt sawàat khaàt jai   สุดสวาทขาดใจ

This romantic heart phrase is used to emphasize the depth of one's emotional feelings for another. In written Thai the phrase is found: "*rák khun sùt sawàat khaàt jai*" In other words, "I love you too, too much." Though to use this phrase in a conversation today might cause a native Thai speaker to think, among other things, that one had just emerged from the very distant past, speaking ancient Thai.

Tie Heart

phùuk jai   ผูกใจ

Tie as in tying of the lace of a shoe. In this case, the heart phrase signifies the tying together of two hearts. So how does one persuade another to tie their heart to one's own? A simple answer is the person through actions makes another love them. By being loyal, faithful, witty, patient, compassionate, one can usually succeed in tying another's heart to their own. Alternatively, if one does not possess such lofty qualities of character, one might try making gifts of a Rolex, BMW, and penthouse condo. Or cash or gold can also create a tie. Whether the heart tied with gold is as well "tied" as one tied with the qualities mentioned above is beyond the scope of this book.

Utmost Heart

sùt khûa hǔa jai   สุดขั้วหัวใจ

This romantic phrase is used when lovers wish to express the feeling that their heart is filled to the maximum with love for the other person in their life. "Utmost heart" is a useful phrase to reassure another about one's feelings of devotion and love for her or him. If one's lover is feeling insecure in the relationship, then hearing the phrase *sùt khûa hǔa jai* may allow him or her to overcome the feelings of insecurity.

One Heart

rák jon mòt jai   รักจนหมดใจ

Another expression of love is the concept of one heart. The heart has feelings (and room for) only one person other than oneself. As a romantic heart phrase, it conveys loyalty, devotion and faithfulness to another.

Save in the Heart

kèp jai   เก็บใจ

Someone is saving their heart for another. Someone other than their lover or spouse does not occupy this "saved heart". Lek's boyfriend has gone abroad to study. During the period that he is away in New York, Lek has many guys floating around her, wanting to date her. But she pays them no attention and remains faithful to her boyfriend. She *kèp jai* for her boyfriend.

Studying the Heart

Study the Heart

duu jai   ดูใจ

One studies the heart of his or her lover to determine how sincere they are about the relationship. In this respect, all lovers are students of the heart. The subject of this study includes, in addition to evidence of sincerity, qualities such as loyalty, honesty, kindness, compassion and gentleness. While the act of studying is an ongoing activity, the term is rarely used among lovers. This heart expression is more commonly used by a friend who confesses that he or she is studying the heart of his or her lover. *duu jai* is used as a verb. There is also a second meaning: friends and relatives who look at a dying person's face.

Testing the Heart

Test One's Heart

yàng jai   หยั่งใจ

In matters of the heart, one person will often put the other to the test in order to determine their true feelings and intentions. There may be some doubts as to the nature of the relationship and one person wishes to put this to the test. For instance, Lek and Vinai have been friends for six months. Vinai asks Lek to be his girlfriend; however, she is not really certain about the degree of his commitment and Vinai remains silent on this issue. To put the matter to the test, Lek accepts a date with Worachai. Soon after discovering Worachai's interest in Lek, Vinai proposes that they become engaged.

Truth and Trust

It is natural to wish to convey how important truth and trust are in a relationship. Issues such as truth-telling, certainty of feeling, loyalty, sincerity, and compatibility are at the heart of any relationship. In this section, the required vocabulary to provide these necessary emotional assurances are set forth.

At Heart

trong hŭa jai   ตรงหัวใจ

One lover expresses feelings to the object of his or her love. If the expression is one of love, the listener will feel happy. On the other hand, if a husband says he hates his wife, this will likely cause her to feel unhappy. She feels happy or sad in heart. The heart phrase *trong hŭa jai* means the place where one feels their happiness or sadness.

Compatible Heart

thùuk jai   ถูกใจ

Two people enjoy the same movies, books, wine, and friends. They are compatible in their world view, their outlook and taste. They feel a sense of common ground when their lover gives them exactly the right gift at the right time; that sense that she or he knows and understands their taste, desires, and wants because they are shared with her or him.

One Heart

jai deaw   ใจเดียว

The man or woman who is and remains faithful to his or her partner is *jai deaw*. Every lover's dream is to find the partner who only has eyes for him or her. This is the Thai way of expressing that desire of "one woman, one man". The importance of this heart phrase can not be over-emphasized. Thais dislike being set up with phony expectations. If one promises to be *jai deaw*, their lover will likely question them, test them, do everything in their power to see if they are serious. The indiscriminate use of "one heart" can create a balloon of expectation that when it goes, it may be with a bang and not a whimper.

Sure Heart

nÊE jai   แน่ใจ

In a relationship, where one is certain of his or her feelings towards the other, he or she is *nÊE jai*. This is the feeling of being sure. In other contexts, it may be used to signal certainty. One has no doubt about making a decision such as buying a new shirt or studying Thai.

True Heart

jing jai   จริงใจ

A person who expresses his or her true feelings of love, caring, or considerations to another is *jing jai*. The essence is sincerity of feeling. There is no mask or deceit in the words or behavior of a person who is *jing jai*. The heart phrase often comes in the form of a question from a Thai speaker. He or she is looking for reassurance. Who isn't? After he or she's heard a hundred pitches, a thousand lies, it is wonderful to think they have enough resilience to even ask, *"khun jing jai rǔue plàw"*. "Are you of true heart or not?" It is a question a lover asks, and then he or she reads your eyes for the answer.

Trust Heart

wáy jai   ไว้ใจ

The element of trusting another is from the heart in Thai. *wáy jai* is the act of trusting. When one trusts another person, they say *wáy jai*. In this heart phrase one is saying, "In my heart I trust you." Trust, in this case, is based on telling the truth, and not deceiving or betraying another who relies on one's words and actions. There isn't a lover alive who doesn't want to trust his or her partner. This is always a question of timing. If the statement comes too soon, it sounds like an obvious lie. If it comes late, it may come too late and your lover has left.

Heart Talk
Hand Talk

Chapter 13

Heart Talk is not limited to spoken language. The deaf in Thailand have their own distinct sign language and culture. And in Thailand, the deaf are a visible and important part of the community. Many of the street vendors found on Silom and Sukhumvit Roads are deaf. This, however, in no way prevents them from expressing heart phrases with the same skill and precision as Thai speakers using the spoken word.

The following selection of Heart Talk sign language will assist you in communicating with this group of Thais who have a highly evolved vocabulary of the heart. In many cases, the influence of spoken and written Thai is apparent and has crossed over into Thai sign language. But there are examples where the sign language and spoken language diverge.

For example, the Thai word *khâw jai*—or understanding— illustrates the absence of separation between the heart and the mind. In spoken and written Thai, *jai* refers to both heart and mind. In the case of sign language, the hand is raised to the head, suggesting that this is the place of understanding. Yet in the Thai sign language, the gesture for "love" is a gesture towards the heart; but in spoken and written Thai *rák* or love is not a *jai* word.

It is outside the scope of this book to explore the intriguing possibility that spoken and written Thai and sign language Thai may, at least in part, have been shaped by different concepts, ideas and influences.

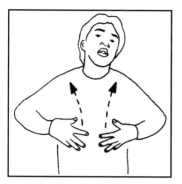

kra yìm jai กระหยิ่มใจ
phOO jai พอใจ
pleasant (generic), satisfied

Note: The long, slow movement is for emphasis of feeling.

hěn jai เห็นใจ
plOOp jai ปลอบใจ

concern, to care for

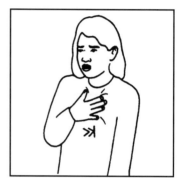

wǎan jai หวานใจ

affection, fondness

sanìt sanam (sanìt jai) สนิทสนม(สนิทใจ)

to be close, to have a supportive relationship, intimate friendship

"Nit and Noi are very close friends."

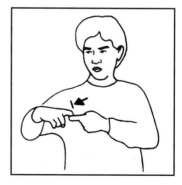

hěn jai เห็นใจ

pity, sympathy These two signs illustrate the dropping of a base hand in two-handed alternating forms, a pattern common in sign languages. These signs are related to signs referring to consoling a person.

hây kamlang jai ให้กำลังใจ

to support, encourage

taam jai ตามใจ

whatever, whichever, anything will do, either is acceptable

The signs on this page use alternating movements. Notice also that in English and other spoken languages we "weigh" alternatives. TSL is using the same metaphor.

khâw jai เข้าใจ

understand

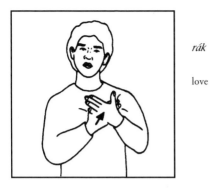

rák รัก

love

wáy jai ไว้ใจ

believe, trust

tòk long jai ตกลงใจ

accept, agree, okay

phOO jai พอใจ

satisfied, fulfilled. The movement in this sign ends in a stop contrasting with the preceding sign. The next sign has repeated movement. Notice differences.

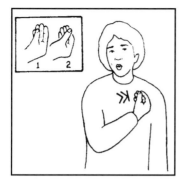

rÓOnjai ร้อนใจ

worried, anxious

The sign has a repeated tapping on the body indicated by the symbol in the drawing. At the same time there is a rubbing of the thumb over the fingers, referring to a last heartbeat. There is one rub for each tap.

mâymânjai ไม่มั่นใจ

don't want to, no confidence in (from fear or misgivings), no desire to

This sign combines several meanings: Lack of confidence, trepidation, lack of desire, and no interest in (going, doing, etc.)

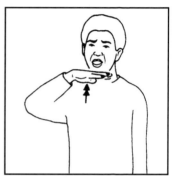

mâychûeajaituaeeng ไม่เชื่อใจตัวเอง
mâymânjai ไม่มั่นใจ

diffidence, overwhelmed (apprehensive of situation), overawed (intimidated by task or situation)
"It'd be the end of me!"
(Used as an exclamation in a situation the speaker feels is overwhelming.)

yàakuanjai อย่ากวนใจ

don't bother me (with idle talk), to cut off. A person who is a nuisance.

tìt yùu nay jai ติดอยู่ในใจ

remember carefully, retain in one's memory, fix in one's mind

tàt sǐn jai mây dâay ตัดสินใจไม่ได้

indecision (from too many conflicting choices),
vacillate (can't pick one option over another),
waiver (between choices or options)

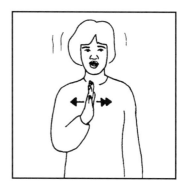

wáy jai mây dâay ไว้ใจไม่ได้

led astray from duty easily, uncertain, unsure of duty or responsibility, vacillate

cèp jai เจ็บใจ, *khÉEn jai* แค้นใจ

rancor, hard feelings, umbrage, pique

cèp jai เจ็บใจ

rancor, hold a grudge, angry heart

mây cèp jai ไม่เจ็บใจ, *mây khÉEn jai* ไม่แค้นใจ

no rancor, not angry

A negation formed by a compound with the sign "don't have."

cèp jai เจ็บใจ

heartache

This sign refers to an emotional hurt, not a physical one.

jai ráay ใจร้าย
jai leew ใจเลว
jai saam ใจทราม

badhearted, wicked

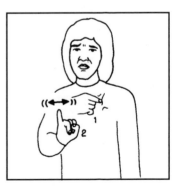

nÔOk jai นอกใจ
jai mii lǎay hÔOng ใจมีหลายห้อง
sǑOng jai สองใจ

polygamy, polyandry, to have many wives/
husbands

jai loo lee ใจโลเล

promiscuous

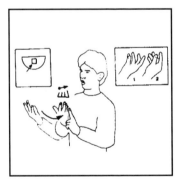

jai loo lee ใจโลเล

to be promiscuous (I am)

hǔa jai waay หัวใจวาย
khàat jai ขาดใจ

This sign is done quickly to show the
sudden nature of a heart attack.

hŭa jai tên rEEng หัวใจเต้นแรง

pounding heart, heart beats strongly

This sign has a repeated opening of the fingertips from under the thumb.

jai tên ใจเต้น

palpitation of the heart, heart beats rapidly

This sign has a repeated opening of the fingertips from under the thumb. The openings are smaller and more than in the sign above.

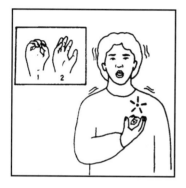

jai sŭung ใจสูง

high-minded, well-educated, high- level thoughts

khÒOp jai ขอบใจ

thank you

kreengjai   เกรงใจ

reticent, reluctant to impose, consideration
for (others, situation)

The facial expression indicates awe. The
movement usually occurs once.

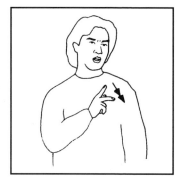

kreengjai   เกรงใจ

reticent, reluctant to impose, consideration
for (others, situation)

A

B

C

T

U

V

W

Z